LONDON COUNTRY BUS HAND

Nicholas King

C000054560

Capital Transport

First published 1998
ISBN 185414 197 X

Published by
Capital Transport Publishing, Harrow Weald

Printed by
CS Graphics, Singapore

Contents

Introduction and Review of 1997

This book gives details at January 1998 of the bus fleets of the main operators surrounding Greater London (corresponding to the former London Country Bus Services area), together with a summary of vehicles used on Green Line services.

The author gratefully acknowledges the assistance of many of the operators concerned. Particular help has been given by Peter Nichols, David Stewart, and officers of the London Omnibus Traction Society and the PSV Circle.

Four of these operators included in this book – County Bus, Kentish Bus, London & Country and The Shires – now form part of Arriva Passenger Services, the new name for the former Cowie Group plc. Over the next few years the attractive local liveries which had been developed by these companies, accompanied by local marketing names, will be replaced by the corporate Arriva livery of aquamarine with off-white front upperwork. In all four fleets, extensive fleet modernisation has continued during 1997, led by substantial injections of low-floor vehicles and new-generation midibuses. The Shires introduced a new fleet numbering system in March 1997, replacing the two schemes which had derived from the former London Country North West and Luton & District operations. At the end of November 1997, Kentish Bus fleet numbers were brought into the Maidstone & District series, reflecting the common management organisation which has been in place for the past two years.

1997 saw a certain amount of operational reorganisation amongst the former Cowie companies, a process completed in January 1998. The central London operations of Kentish Bus were parcelled off to Leaside and South London (including some balancing transfers of work with Stagecoach Selkent). In addition, London & Country undertook major revisions of their network during the summer of 1997. In October 1997, County Bus took over the Leaside Travel private hire and contract operation at their resited Edmonton depot.

In June 1997 East Surrey was purchased by Metrobus of Orpington. Vehicles have quickly received Metrobus-style liveries, and what is now Metrobus East Surrey also oversees the South Coast operation which Metrobus introduced in July 1997 following the collapse of Leisurelink.

Speedlink Airport Services have continued to improve the age profile of vehicles used on their network of services linking London airports, and have assumed operation of the Heathrow FastTrain bus link between airport terminals and a temporary station near Stockley Park for the Heathrow Express train link to and from Paddington.

January 1998   NICHOLAS KING

Front cover: The ten Dennis Arrows with East Lancs bodywork delivered to London & Country in 1996 seem destined to remain a unique batch. AD10 carries upper-deck advertising for Countryliner facilities. *Gerald Mead*

Back cover: High Wycombe is the home for all Leyland Atlanteans in The Shires' fleet on account of their hill-climbing performance. No.5040, bodied by Roe, basks in the sun in July 1997. *Colin Brown*

Page 1: At the end of 1995 Kentish Bus received ten Scania L113CRL vehicles with low-floor Wright bodywork for route 480. Kent County Council provided financial support for the venture. No.256 (now 3256) represents the type. *Laurie Rufus*

Page 2: Eight Dennis Darts with Carlyle bodywork were delivered to what was then London Country North West in 1991. No.3096 received Lucketts fleetnames in 1997 following the purchase of that firm. *Peter Newman*

Page 3: Amongst 28 Iveco Turbo Daily minibuses with Marshall bodywork delivered to County Bus in 1994/5 is MB725. These have proved to be the last Ivecos delivered to the company. *David Heath*

Left: One of the attractive liveries to disappear over the next few years is carried by Greenway National 364, seen shortly after repainting into Guildford & West Surrey livery in June 1997 at Esher. *Geoff Rixon*

Above right: An early repaint into Arriva livery is Kent Thameside 5766, a Leyland Olympian new to Boro'line Maidstone in 1991, seen at Bexleyheath on an LT contract route. *D. Heath*

Right: Metrobus East Surrey bought three Dennis Darts with Wadham Stringer bodywork from Eastbourne Buses in 1997 following its expansion into new territory. *David Harman*

ARRIVA

Arriva Passenger Services is the new name introduced from 1st January 1998 for the bus operations of the former Cowie Group plc. The change of name, which was approved by shareholders in November 1997, forms part of an overall rebranding of the group, under which bus and coach operation is now marketed as Arriva Bus and Coach, the motor dealership network as Arriva Motor Retailing, and vehicle management as Arriva Automotive Solutions. A new corporate livery of aquamarine designed by Best Impressions is being introduced on buses. On single-deckers, there is an off-white, officially 'Champagne', area at the front above skirt level, continuing around each side to curve up to the roof behind the front axle. On double-deckers, the off-white area adopts a similar position on the upper-deck. A thin white line divides these two colours, and a yellow coachline is carried around the vehicle at mid-skirt height. White Arriva logos are carried on the sides, together with a local marketing strapline. The County Bus strapline is "serving Herts & Essex", that for Kentish Bus is "serving Kent Thameside", that for The Shires is "serving the Shires", and for London & Country the strapline is "serving Surrey & West Sussex". This new livery will replace existing local liveries but dedicated operations, such as Green Line, will retain their present liveries.

The management of Arriva companies within the area covered by this book has been increasingly rationalised during 1997. County Bus is now responsible for oversight of Arriva operations in Colchester and Southend, whilst Kentish Bus has been managed from Maidstone (within the Invictaway group) since October 1995. Management of London & Country, is gradually moving from Reigate to Maidstone, with some local responsibilities being established at Crawley. On 1st January 1998 the residual central London operations of Kentish Bus were transferred to Leaside, and with the closing of the Dunton Green garage on 14th February 1998, the Kent Thameside division will be reduced to just two garages, at Dartford and Northfleet, with a small outstation at Tonbridge.

Above: The Arriva brandings replace respectively County Bus, Kentish Bus, London & Country and The Shires.

Left: The first batch of new vehicles for the Arriva companies covered in this book to carry the new corporate livery was of ten Dennis Darts allocated to Watford garage. No.3207 is seen at Rickmansworth in January. *David Stewart*

ARRIVA HERTS & ESSEX (COUNTY BUS)

County Bus and Coach Co Ltd, Bus Garage, Harlow, Essex, CM20 1DU

London Country North East was privatised to the AJS Group from April 1988. County Bus and Coach Ltd was established in January 1989 as the eastern part with its head office in Harlow. The Company was sold to the Lynton Travel Group in July 1991 and re-sold in October 1994 to West Midlands Travel. In February 1996 the Company was sold again, this time to the Cowie Group plc. This was renamed to Arriva in November 1997. Under the rationalisation of the group's operations in the South East, County Bus assumed organisational control of Colchester and Southend Transport in June 1997.

The County name is not carried on vehicles. Instead, the trading names of Town Link, Lea Valley and Thameside are used for Harlow and Debden, Ware and Edmonton, and Grays respectively. In the past two years the company has invested heavily in fleet modernisation resulting in many new vehicles, especially Dennis Darts, joining the fleet. In August 1997 the bus work of West, Woodford Green was taken over, and in October 1997 Edmonton depot took over the Leaside Travel operation of Leaside Buses.

Routes are operated in Essex and Hertfordshire, together with LT contract routes including most of the north-east London Mobility Bus network.

The fleet carries cream and green livery, and is based at Debden (Langston Road), Edmonton (Lea Valley Trading Estate), Grays (Europa Park), Harlow (Fourth Avenue) and Ware (Marsh Lane).

1994 saw the purchase of four low-floor Dennis Lances with Wright Pathfinder bodywork. ELW269, the last of the order, runs through Epping in August 1997. *Richard Godfrey*

In dedicated livery for routes 310/310A, DIB927 is a DAF SB220 with Ikarus bodywork new in 1992 to Grey-Green, passing to County Bus in 1997. It was caught at Waltham Cross in April 1997 when it was still classified DI. The classification was changed to avoid a clash with DI coaches of Leaside Travel. *Richard Godfrey*

Below: From a batch of eleven standard 9m Dennis Darts with Plaxton bodywork purchased in 1996, DP325 is seen in Waycross Road, Upminster in September of that year. *Keith Wood*

Left: County Bus have adopted a red-based livery for their Hertford Road operations. Roe-bodied Leyland Olympian LR7, one of thirteen vehicles in such livery, was found on a southbound trip to Enfield on the revised 310 corridor in April 1997. *Gerald Mead*

Right: On the same route at Cecil Road, Enfield in September 1997 was MCW Metrobus M9, recently transferred from Leaside. This vehicle had started life with Greater Manchester. *Mike Harris*

In 1990, County Bus purchased eight new Leyland Lynxes. LX254 was seen on the 201 near Ivychimneys. Two further Lynxes arrived from Grey-Green in 1996. *Nick Malony*

The turn of the decade saw the delivery of Mercedes-Benz 709D minibuses with Reeve Burgess and Plaxton bodywork. The route branding on MB930 might easily be mistaken for a fleet number at first glance in this view at Cheshunt in April 1997. *Richard Godfrey*

Facing page: An unusual purchase in 1993 was a quartet of Peugeot-Talbot minibuses with tail-lifts. In 1994, MBT805 followed as a fifth, being photographed at Waltham Cross. *Mike Harris*

County Bus was one of the last major operators to receive Dormobile-bodied vehicles, when six Iveco Turbo midibuses were delivered in 1993. MB711 is seen at Harlow. *Nick Malony*

MB154 is a more usual Iveco Daily with Reeve Burgess bodywork purchased in 1989 after a year as a demonstrator. Posing for the camera at Waltham Cross in April 1997, it is fitted with high-back seating. *Richard Godfrey*

Four Iveco Turbo Daily vehicles were bought in 1994 with Marshall bodywork including facilities for the disabled, and are used on LT Mobility Bus routes. MBT714 was found at Stratford Broadway. *Mike Harris*

The first of fifteen Mercedes-Benz Varios with Plaxton bodywork due with County Bus at the end of 1997 was displayed at the Bus & Coach Show in Birmingham during October 1997. Delay in delivery of these vehicles may result in them being given Arriva livery before entering service. *Capital Transport*

ARRIVA KENT THAMESIDE (KENTISH BUS)

Kentish Bus & Coach Co Ltd, Invicta House, Armstrong Road, Maidstone, Kent, ME15 6TY

Kentish Bus & Coach was re-named from London Country South East on 27th April 1987, and purchased by the Proudmutual Group, later part of British Bus. British Bus was itself bought out by the Cowie group in June 1996, of which the shareholders approved a change of title to Arriva in November 1997. Management has been conducted from Maidstone since October 1995 alongside that of Maidstone & District, with whom there are increasingly-close operational links. In November 1997 the Kent-based fleet was renumbered into a common series with M&D.

Kentish Bus operate a mixture of commercial and Kent County Council services in north west Kent, together with a number of LT contracts including Mobility Bus services in the Croydon area. From January 1995 some of the LT work was taken over by the newly-formed Londonlinks company, and all such work within Greater London was transferred to associated operators by January 1998 except the Mobility Bus network in the Croydon area.

The present livery is green and yellow, though some vehicles still carry the older livery of primrose yellow with maroon relief. Arriva livery of aquamarine with off-white upper frontwork will be replacing both varieties in the coming months. Vehicles are based at Dartford and Northfleet.

When Kentish Bus took over the LT work of Boro'line Maidstone in February 1992, sixteen Leyland Lynxes formed part of the transferred fleet. No.406 (now 3059) had received the smart new livery when photographed in July 1997. *John Miller*

Facing page: In the spring of 1997, Kentish Bus route 12 was renumbered 498 and converted to low-floor Dennis Dart operation, using a batch of six buses with Plaxton bodywork. No.186 (now 3186) was on its way to the eastern end of the route in August 1997. *John Miller*

RIVERVIEW PARK
Perry Street Denton
498
Step-Free Entrance means
EASY ACCESS
for pushchairs
EASY ACCESS
for shoppers
EASY ACCESS
for everyone
186
Kentishbus
186
Kentishbus
PLAXTON
DENNIS
P186 LKJ

At the end of 1995, route 480 was converted to low-floor Scanias with Wright Access Ultralow bodywork. No.252 (now 3252) was caught at Dartford in June 1996. *Laurie Rufus*

Boro'line Maidstone received eleven Leyland Olympians with Optare bodywork in 1988 for LT work. A twelfth, No.762 (now 5762) followed in 1989, and was photographed at Dartford still in 'London' livery in October 1996. *Laurie Rufus*

Ten Volvo Citybuses with East Lancs bodywork were shared between Kentish Bus and Londonlinks when they came south from North Western in 1996. No.7702 represents the type at Bexleyheath in January 1998. *D. Heath*

Fourteen Volvo Citybuses with Alexander bodywork were purchased in 1989 by Boro'line Maidstone for LT work, passing to Kentish Bus in 1992. Three are now in Kent, and of these No.722 (now 7722) was seen at Bexleyheath in September 1997. *Laurie Rufus*

Facing page: Amongst the large order for Volvo Citybuses with Northern Counties bodies received by London Country South West in 1989, several later made their way to Londonlinks. No.634 (now 7634) was further transferred to Kentish Bus when those services were rationalised in 1996/7, and was seen at Biggin Hill in October 1997. Route 320 passed from Kentish Bus to Stagecoach Selkent in November. *Richard Godfrey*

The oldest Leyland Atlantean remaining in service with Kentish Bus is AN172 (now 6172), new in 1979 with Park Royal bodywork. September 1997 found it at Bexleyheath on a school service. *Laurie Rufus*

The last Kentish Bus Leyland National to receive Greenway treatment from East Lancs in 1994, No.362 (now 3362) had started life with London Country at Reigate in 1978. Here it is seen at Sidcup in August 1997. *Laurie Rufus*

The most recent midibus deliveries to Kentish Bus are eight Optare MetroRiders which arrived in 1996. No.805 (now 1805) at Orpington represents a type of which the outward appearance has changed little in its ten years of production. *Stephen Madden*

In December 1996 Kentish Bus took over operation of the Crossways Business Park service, acquiring No.895 (now 1154) for the purpose. It is a Mercedes-Benz 814D of 1992 with Dormobile bodywork. The blue circle on the livery is a reference to the former sponsor of Crossways – Blue Circle Industries. *Laurie Rufus*

ARRIVA SURREY & WEST SUSSEX (LONDON & COUNTRY)

Gem Fairtax (1991) Ltd, Lesbourne Road, Reigate, Surrey, RH2 7LE
Guildford and West Surrey Buses Ltd, Lesbourne Road, Reigate, Surrey, RH7 2LE
Horsham Buses Ltd, Lesbourne Road, Reigate, Surrey, RH2 7LE
London & Country Ltd, Lesbourne Road, Reigate, Surrey, RH2 7LE

London & Country was renamed from London Country Bus South West early in 1993, having been privatised to the Drawlane group in February 1988. Drawlane became British Bus in December 1992. In June 1996 British Bus was itself purchased by the Cowie group, which was renamed Arriva in November 1997. Gem Fairtax, Guildford & West Surrey and Horsham Buses are separate operating identities within the group, each with its own operator authorisation, but there is considerable interchange between these and the parent fleets, and the group is therefore given as one here. The former operations at Croydon, Walworth and Dunton Green, chiefly on LT contracts, were transferred to the newly-formed Londonlinks company on 1st January 1995. During the second half of 1997 there was further rationalisation within the then Cowie group's south-eastern portfolio which led to oversight of the residual Londonlinks operation reverting to London & Country. Some administrative functions are now carried out by the Invictaway group at Maidstone.

The livery is light green with dark green and red relief, and the fleet operates from bases at Cranleigh, Crawley, Guildford, Hounslow, Leatherhead, Merstham, Slyfield, Warnham and Woking.

The successor to the Dennis Dominator, the Arrow, found early favour with London & Country. AD6, with 80-seat bodywork by East Lancs, was found in Morden on route 420 in April 1997. *Geoff Rixon*

Facing page: Volvo Olympians are rare in the London & Country fleet. No.703, with East Lancs body, was one of four delivered in 1994, and was photographed at Kingston in August 1997. *Geoff Rixon*

London & Country turned to the Dennis Dominator at the very end of its production life. DD16, new in 1996 with East Lancs bodywork, was the last new one delivered to the operator.
Gerald Mead

An earlier Dennis Dominator, also bodied by East Lancs was DD6, one of seven new in 1989, and seen in August 1997.
Geoff Rixon

Amongst the relatively small number of Leyland Olympians in stock is LR29, new in 1982 with Roe bodywork. It was seen in Kingston in July 1997 following the major revision of services in that area. *Geoff Rixon*

Left: Once a major user of Leyland Atlanteans, London & Country still have a number in stock. One of the latest is AN285 with Roe bodywork, photographed in Staines in October 1997. *Colin Brown*

Right: Four Leyland Olympians with Northern Counties bodywork passed from Kentish Bus to London & Country in 1992 when only three years old. LR503 was found in Kingston showing a Green Line blind in July 1997. *Stephen Madden*

Facing page: Five low-floor Dennis Lances joined the fleet in 1995 for the conversion of route 408. LSL9, the last of them, demonstrates the Wright Pathfinder body with which they were equipped. *Stephen Madden*

Left: Large quantities of low-floor Dennis Darts have arrived in the past eighteen months. DSL84 is one of 41 received in 1997, and was approaching Kingston Bridge in July 1997. The simplified livery, with less of the dark green, will be noted. *Geoff Rixon*

Unique in the fleet is VCB89, a Volvo B10M of 1986 with Caetano Stagecoach bodywork, acquired in 1995 from Tellings-Golden Miller. This vehicle is now normally only to be found on school or contract work in the Guildford area. *Stephen Madden*

451 Weybridge Byfleet
WOKING

London & Country

London & Country

JIL 2197

To help with fleet modernisation, London & Country underwent a major programme of having Leyland Nationals rebuilt to Greenway specification by East Lancs from 1992 to 1995. No.357, originally a Southdown vehicle, was one of the earliest of the type when new in 1973. *Stephen Madden*

Above: Typifying the standard Dennis Dart with East Lancs bodywork which formed the backbone of single-deck intake from 1993 to 1996 is DS20 in Portsmouth Road, Kingston. *Geoff Rixon*

Left: Fifteen Dennis Lances with East Lancs bodywork were purchased in 1996 to help in replacing a backlog of older vehicles. LS10, seen at Crawley, represents the type. *Malc McDonald*

Facing page: Whilst in British Bus ownership, London & Country was a major customer for East Lancs bodywork, such as shown on low-floor Dennis Dart DSL54 at Roffey in September 1997. *Richard Godfrey*

The sole Optare MetroRider in the fleet, MR472 was delivered in 1996 for London Transport work, and was found at Kingston Hospital in October 1997.
Geoff Rixon

In special livery for the Gatwick Airporter service, No. 466 (carrying fleet number MM466) is a Mercedes-Benz 709D with Plaxton bodywork, and was tracked down at Gatwick in September 1997.
Richard Godfrey

In 1989, a number of coaches were acquired from Shamrock & Rambler, including SR90, a Leyland Tiger with Plaxton coachwork. With livery adapted for Countryliner work, it was caught at Trafalgar Square in July 1996.
Stephen Madden

Another of the Leyland Tigers acquired from Shamrock & Rambler in 1989, SR88 carries standard livery with grey skirt in this view at Crawley in September 1997.
Richard Godfrey

ARRIVA THE SHIRES

LDT Ltd, Castle Street, Luton, LU1 3AJ

The Shires emanates from the former Luton & District and London Country North West fleets. The latter was taken over by the former in October 1990, and has taken over services from a number of other local operators subsequently. These include Stuart Palmer of Dunstable in October 1994, Buffalo Bus of Flitwick in May 1995, Motts (Yellow Bus) of Aylesbury in July 1995, Lucketts of Watford in January 1997 and Checker of Garston in April 1997. Vehicles acquired from these operators have added an eclectic element to a varied fleet, including Leyland Swifts, more Iveco minibuses and Bristol VRTs, and a quantity of Volvo coaches. In October 1997 a new marketing initiative was introduced in Luton under the Challenger fleetname.

Luton & District had been taken over by British Bus in July 1994, and passed to the ownership of the Cowie Group in June 1996. This was in turn renamed Arriva in November 1997. The present local marketing names were introduced in April 1995, coupled with the adoption of the present registered name and a new livery of blue and yellow with a grey skirt. This livery has almost entirely replaced the former Brunswick green and cargo grey of the LCNW-derived fleet and the red and cream of the L&D era. Both are now to be replaced by the new Arriva livery of aquamarine with off-white front upperwork.

The fleet, which was completely renumbered in March 1997, operates from depots at Aylesbury, Dunstable, Hemel Hempstead, High Wycombe, Hitchin, Luton, Stevenage and Watford (Garston and Tolpits Lane), with outstations at Amersham and Leighton Buzzard.

A number of Scanias based at Aylesbury and Hemel Hempstead carry route branding for the 500. No.3165 loads at Watford in July 1997. *Colin Brown*

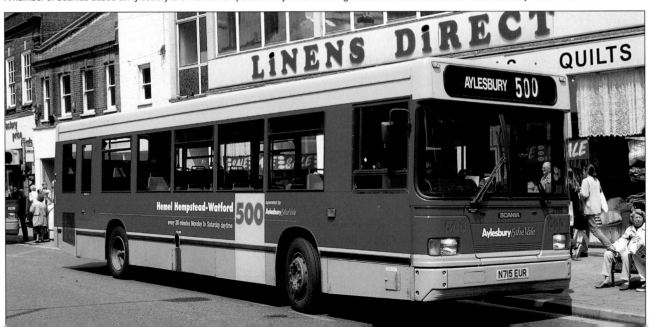

The Shires fleet contains four Leyland Olympians with 83-seat Northern Counties bodywork which had been sold by Ensign within a year of build. All are allocated to High Wycombe, where No.5135 was encountered at Castle Street in April 1997. *Colin Brown*

No.5092 comes from a batch of twelve Leyland Olympians bodied by Alexander in 1988. Here it loads at Watford in April 1997 before returning to Hemel Hempstead. *Colin Brown*

Amongst the Leyland Olympians with Eastern Coach Works bodywork which were new to London Country, No.5076 reached The Shires from Sovereign rather than through local retention. It was photographed at High Wycombe in July 1997. *Colin Brown*

Bristol VRTs with Eastern Coach Works bodies are not common in the area, but The Shires still hold several, most of which were inherited from United Counties with Luton area services in 1986. No.5019 poses for the camera in August 1997. *Gerald Mead*

Facing page: No.5017, seen at Croxley Green in May 1997, originated with South Wales and was re-registered in 1996. Its livery shows that its main use on college days is on services serving West Herts College at Watford. *Colin Brown*

Above: The fleet includes 27 Scania L113 vehicles with East Lancs bodywork. No.3160 is another vehicle primarily intended for West Herts College service, though caught here on other work in September 1996.
Capital Transport

In 1994, thirty-two Volvo B6 single-deckers with Northern Counties bodywork were received. No.3126 (then still carrying its former fleet number of 326) carries dedicated route branding for Heathrow services 74 and 75, which are marketed jointly with Bee Line.
Malcolm King

Despite the Volvo badging, No.3052, originally a United Counties vehicle, carries a DAF engine. This view was taken at Rickmansworth when the vehicle was on hire to Lucketts of Watford, whose services were subsequently taken over by The Shires. *Colin Brown*

Facing page: Twenty low-floor Dennis Darts were ordered for 1996/7, to be bodied by East Lancs. The first four were bodied as originally ordered and these went to Hemel Hempstead, as represented by No.3173 at Bridge Street in May 1997. *Colin Brown*

Below: The other sixteen of the order were, in the event, bodied by Plaxton following the change to Cowie ownership. No.3185 displays route branding for the 348 at Woodside in April 1997. *Richard Godfrey*

Several Leyland Nationals rebuilt by East Lancs to Greenway specification were acquired from Crosville Wales in 1995. No.3054 was tracked down at Stevenage in April 1997. *Colin Brown*

The first Dennis Darts in the fleet arrived in 1991 with Carlyle bodywork. No.3094 stands beneath the trees in Watford town centre in July 1997. *Colin Brown*

Four of the sixteen Leyland Lynxes in the fleet (from various sources) have high-backed seating. No.3068 was at Croxley Green in May 1997; the 321 now only reaches that point in the evenings and on Sundays. *Colin Brown*

Somewhat surprising was the arrival of five Dennis Darts with Wright bodywork in 1994. All were sent to Hemel Hempstead, where No.3090 had arrived on the rural route from Watford in May 1997. *Colin Brown*

Above: Substantial numbers of Mercedes-Benz 709Ds with Plaxton bodywork arrived in 1995/6. They included 2115 for the Elstree & Borehamwood operation and 2132, which carries dedicated livery for the Hemel Hempstead Park & Ride service.
Capital Transport/Colin Brown

Left: Acquired from Buffalo, Flitwick in 1995 was No.2067, a Mercedes-Benz 709D with Carlyle bodywork. It was found in Milton Keynes Central Bus Station in September 1997. *Malc McDonald*

Whilst the demotion of former coaches to bus work is not uncommon, the repainting of No.4006 into bus livery was an unexpected step. A Leyland Tiger of 1983 with Plaxton coachwork, this view was taken at Abbots Langley in August 1997. *Nick Malony*

A very unusual vehicle acquired from Lucketts in 1997 was No.4037, a Dennis Javelin with UVG coachwork, seen at Garston in August 1997 still carrying a version of Lucketts livery. *John G.S. Smith*

THE BEE LINE

Berks Bucks Bus Co Ltd, Macmillan House, Paddington Station, London W2 1TY

The present company arose from the division of the former Thames Valley & Aldershot Omnibus Company Ltd on 1st January 1986, when it was named Alder Valley North. Becoming Berks Bucks Bus Co in January 1987, it was sold by the NBC to Q Drive, part of the Len Wright group, in December 1987. Operations in the High Wycombe area were transferred to Oxford Bus Company in November 1990. The Londonlink service went to Reading Transport in October 1991 and operations at Newbury and Reading followed in July 1992. Work in the Slough area was taken over from Luton & District in January 1993. The most recent change of ownership took place on 20th March 1996, when the operation was sold to the CentreWest group, who were subsequently purchased by FirstBus (now FirstGroup). They have retained its separate identity. The operational area corresponds in part with that of the former Thames Valley Traction Company.

The current livery is bright yellow with blue skirt and orange stripes. The fleet is operated from depots at Bracknell and Slough.

Amongst eight Dennis Darts with Plaxton bodywork delivered to The Bee Line in 1993/4 is L206, displaying attractive route dedicated livery including FirstBus logos at Langley in October 1997. *Capital Transport*

Low-floor vehicles made their appearance with The Bee Line in 1996, when seven Dennis Darts were delivered with Plaxton bodywork. L216 pauses at Hyde Park Corner on its way to Windsor while substituting on a Green Line service. *Capital Transport*

In 1995, ten Scania L113 buses with high-capacity Plaxton bodies were purchased. SN811 was photographed in Reading on one of the type's regular services. This vehicle was built as left-hand-drive but modified for UK use. *Malcolm King*

Five Leyland Lynxes which started their life with Len Wright in 1987 are now in the Bee Line fleet. LX803, the first of the batch, loads at Slough in April 1997. *Colin Brown*

Double-deckers in the Bee Line fleet are very much in the minority. No.504 is one of five Northern Counties bodied Olympians dating from 1988. *Colin Lloyd*

Photographed like 504 at Heathrow Airport, the next Olympian in the batch carries a promotional livery for the airport and is usually to be found on the service between here and Reading. *Nick Malony*

Facing page: No fewer than 49 Renault-Dodge midibuses with Wright bodywork have been transferred from CentreWest during the past year to replace older vehicles. RW7 stands at Slough in April 1997. *Colin Brown*

Above: One of Bee Line's Darts is in dedicated livery for Legoland in Windsor, on the site of the former safari park. During the winter months the bus, L212, can be found on normal bus services. *Nick Malony*

Left: A batch of eight Scanias with Berkhof Excellence 1000 bodywork maintains the popular link to Heathrow from Reading, the interchange point for the rail network from the South West and South Wales. *Nick Malony*

GREEN LINE

Green Line branding is used for a number of coach services which operate from the Home Counties into central London. These have chiefly been the prerogative of the former London Country companies. However, this branding is also used by Maidstone & District and Southend Transport, both members of the Arriva group of companies.

Maidstone & District began to use the Green Line name in 1995 for their network of routes from the Medway Towns and Maidstone, formerly marketed from its inception in 1980 as Invictaway. In May 1997 the Medway Towns routes were transferred to London Coaches (Kent), leaving weekday operations from Maidstone with a peak requirement of eleven vehicles. This service was upgraded in January 1998 with the arrival of new vehicles.

Southend Transport's operation, of similar vintage, was similarly brought under the Green Line banner in 1995. At one stage this comprised through routes to and from Reading, jointly-operated with Reading Buses.

In 1996, Sovereign purchased three new Volvo B10M vehicles with Plaxton Premiere coachwork for the 797 service, which then ran between London and Cambridge. In November 1997 this route was withdrawn north of Baldock in consequence of sustained competition from Express Shuttle. *Capital Transport*

A major part of Green Line work for The Shires is the group of routes which links London with the Hemel Hempstead area. No.4017, a Leyland Tiger with Berkhof coachwork, was originally used on airport services. *Stephen Madden*

At the end of 1997, the high-profile service 757 between Victoria and Luton Airport was restocked with ten new DAF/Plaxton coaches with Première 320 bodywork. The route is worked by The Shires, whose No.4054 is seen at Bricket Wood in December. The coach carries the latest version of Green Line logo and livery. *David Stewart*

Maidstone & District have also renewed much of their residual Green Line network between London and the Maidstone area, using vehicles identical to the design shown above. No.2846, a Volvo B10M with Plaxton coachwork, is one of three older vehicles to remain and heads home in October 1997. *Stephen Madden*

Southend's fleet for Green Line work includes five Leyland Tigers of 1984 with Duple coachwork. No. 547 was on its way home one day in July 1997.
Stephen Madden

The Bee Line's Green Line network is marketed as Londonlink. SB746 is a Scania K113 of 1991 with Berkhof coachwork, seen in the Strand. Rather unusually, the destination is shown on a dot-matrix display low in the nearside front windscreen. *Capital Transport*

Facing page: Former private hire coaches have sometimes been transferred to Green Line work in later life. The Shires' No.4020, a Leyland Tiger of 1988 with Plaxton coachwork, is an example and is seen at Knightsbridge. At one point in their careers, these vehicles were classified STL. *Capital Transport*

Left: A batch of nine low-floor DAF SB220s has been introduced by County Bus in a long-awaited upgrade of the long interurban 724. They are the first Plaxton Prestige bodies in the Home Counties and have large standing and luggage areas to cope with their dual role as a local service in Hertfordshire and a link to Heathrow Airport. PDL202 is seen at Heathrow in December 1997. *Malcolm King*

In 1994, London & Country were well in the throes of a programme of having Leyland Nationals rebuilt to Greenway specification by East Lancs. Some received high-backed seating for Green Line work, such as No.373, which in its original form had been new to Midland Red in 1976. Already standing outside the formal Green Line network when this view was taken in August 1997, the 415 was withdrawn east of Kingston in November 1997. *Laurie Rufus*

METROBUS EAST SURREY

Metrobus Ltd, Oak Farm, Farnborough Hill, Orpington, Kent, BR6 6DA

The former firm of East Surrey Buses was purchased by Metrobus, Orpington in June 1997, and is now operated as a division of the parent operator. East Surrey had gained a significant profile in local bus work since deregulation, when the name had been adopted by Walter, Waddon, and developed to include contracts for Kent and Surrey County Councils. Most recently these have included a suite of routes based on Tunbridge Wells, including workings to and from East Grinstead.

The fleet is based chiefly on Dennis and Optare vehicles. In October 1997 the first double-decker was transferred from the Orpington fleet. Fleet livery is being altered from orange and cream to dark blue and yellow, and vehicles are based at South Godstone with an outstation in Edenbridge.

No.24 in the Metrobus East Surrey fleet is an Optare StarRider on Mercedes-Benz 811D chassis. Photographed at Sevenoaks in September 1997, it had already acquired new livery following the change of ownership. *D. Heath*

Facing page: The first Dennis Dart to join what is now the Metrobus East Surrey fleet was No.36, delivered with Wadham Stringer bodywork in 1991. Within two months of the fleet changing hands it had received new livery, as demonstrated here. *Gerald Mead*

SOVEREIGN

Sovereign Bus & Coach Co Ltd, Babbage Road, Stevenage, Hertfordshire, SG1 2EQ

Sovereign was established on 9th January 1989 (at Hatfield), taking over the western part of the former London Country North East. The Stevenage area operations of Jubilee Coaches were purchased on 25th January 1989, and services in the area were soon rationalised. Welwyn Hatfield Line, which had been operating since August 1987 as a result of LCNE withdrawals in the Welwyn Garden City and Hatfield area, was bought out on 10th January 1990, continuing as a subsidiary until early in 1995. Most operations in the Stevenage area were transferred to Luton & District (now part of The Shires) on 20th May 1990. Operations have subsequently spread to the Harrow area, and BTS of Borehamwood has come under the Sovereign wing, renamed as London Sovereign; those operations are covered in the London Bus Handbook.

Within the Blazefield Holdings group, Sovereign also administers Cambridge Coach Services.

The Hertfordshire fleet is based at North Mymms, Stevenage and St Albans. The initial livery of cream with light blue skirt and stripes is now being augmented by a modest black coachline at skirt level on some vehicles. A few vehicles are painted in Welwyn Hatfield line livery, in which red replaces blue.

Volvo B10B low-floor vehicles with Wright bodywork have been used to upgrade routes 300 and 734. No.106, seen at Hatfield, carries route branding for the latter, which was re-routed to Hemel Hempstead in 1996. *Capital Transport*

Whilst all eleven Leyland Olympians in the Sovereign fleet are of LCBS extraction, most have spent a period with Yorkshire members of the Blazefield group. No.40, bodied by Roe, returned from Keighley & District in 1994. *Gerald Mead*

The majority of single-deck requirements are fulfilled by Leyland Lynxes. No.205 is one of seven delivered in 1989 as the first of the type in the fleet. *Gerald Mead*

Left: On extended demonstration to Sovereign during 1997 has been No.501, a low-floor Dennis Dart with Plaxton bodywork, found at St Albans in November 1997. Note the black stripe, a recent addition to the livery scheme. *D. Heath*

Above: The name of the former Welwyn-Hatfield Line subsidiary is kept alive for marketing purposes. In Welwyn-Hatfield Line colours, but with a private registration which reflects the true ownership, No.433 is a Mercedes-Benz 811D with Plaxton bodywork purchased in 1993. *Capital Transport*

Left: Downgraded to staff ferry and ordinary bus work from its former Green Line glory, No.864 is a Leyland Tiger of 1985 with Plaxton coachwork, of the type common to all the London Country fleets at that time. It was found at Stevenage in April 1997. *Colin Brown*

SPEEDLINK

Speedlink Airport Services Ltd, 106/7 Ashdown House, Gatwick Airport, West Sussex, RH6 0JH

Speedlink was set up in October 1989 as a separate company within the Drawlane group, its services to the main London airports having been initiated by London Country South West. In addition to the Flightline, Jetlink and Speedlink services, the company operates the Woking Railair Link, dedicated services for Virgin Atlantic, and the Heathrow Hotel Hoppa service. In 1995, a network of internal services at Heathrow Airport was gained. In January 1998, Speedlink took on operation of the FastTrain bus link between airport terminals and the temporary station near Stockley Park with its rail link to Paddington.

Speedlink is owned by National Express plc. Vehicles carry a variety of liveries specific to the various operations, and are garaged at Crawley (Tinsley Green), Heathrow Airport (Northwood Road) and North Feltham (Armadale Road). A notable feature is that many coaches carry private SAS registrations.

Amongst vehicles carrying dedicated livery for the eponymous Speedlink service between Heathrow and Gatwick is D4, a DAF with high-specification Van Hool coachwork delivered in 1997. *Stephen Madden*

The Flightline service between Gatwick, central London, and Stansted is operated by Volvo B10Ms with Plaxton coachwork of 1990, now the oldest vehicles in the fleet. V17 represents the type. *Stephen Madden*

The Jetlink operation extends from Norwich to Brighton, serving the airports at Stansted, Luton, Heathrow and Gatwick. D13, with private registration, passes through Hatton Cross in September 1997. *Geoff Rixon*

The Heathrow to Woking Railair service is maintained by five Scania K113 vehicles with Van Hool coachwork. S1, the first of the batch, was at Heathrow Central in June 1995. Newer vehicles are now receiving this livery to upgrade the service. *Nick Malony*

Twenty-six Volvo B6LEs with Wright bodywork were delivered in 1997 for the Hotel Hoppa service, linking local hotels with Heathrow terminals. No.237 poses at the Sheraton Skyline hotel in September 1997. *Colin Brown*

One of nineteen DAFs with Plaxton Prestige bodywork built in 1997 for the FastTrain service is seen at Heathrow Airport in January 1998. *K. N. Vincent*

Eight Mercedes-Benz 814D vehicles were fitted with Autobus Classique coachwork in 1996. AC4 was caught at Staines Centre in October 1997 in Virgin Atlantic livery. *Nick Malony*

Low-floor Dennis Lances with Berkhof bodywork are used for inter-terminal connecting services. No.958 was new in 1995. *Malcolm King*

Internal transfers at Heathrow are effected by ten DAF SB220 vehicles with Northern Counties bodywork. No.902 was caught at Heathrow in October 1996. *Colin Lloyd*

UNIVERSITYBUS

Universitybus Ltd, College Lane, Hatfield, Hertfordshire, AL10 9AB

Originally set up to provide services for students and staff to and from the sites of what is now the University of Hertfordshire, an increasing number of routes have been opened to public use, and local authority contracts have been gained to supplement a wide-ranging network of commercial services. An eclectic collection of vehicles has been assembled, including some most unusual Blue Bird vehicles of American origin. The present fleet title was adopted in 1994. Vehicles are based at Comet Way, Hatfield. Fleet numbers previously used have been discontinued.

Highly unusual vehicles in the fleet are four American-build Blue Bird buses, delivered in 1994. M47HUT, the first of the batch, passes Well Hall College at Aldenham in April 1997. It is expected that these vehicles will be withdrawn during 1998. *Tony Wilson*

One of the earlier Marshall Midibuses to be produced, P980PTM remains the only one of the type in the Universitybus fleet. This view was taken at Harpenden in April 1997. *Tony Wilson*

After serving as a demonstrator for Carlyle, Dennis Dart H840NOC reached Universitybus through its earlier npsv operations for Hertfordshire County Council. Now carrying dedicated livery for West Herts College, it was caught at Watford Junction in March 1997.
Colin Brown

Four of the six orthodox Dennis Darts delivered in 1995 carried bodywork by Marshall. They include N424ENM, seen in Welwyn Garden City in February 1997.
Colin Lloyd

The sole Leyland Lynx in the fleet, G472PGE started life with Whitelaw, Stonehouse. In July 1997 it was photographed at Watford. *Colin Brown*

A major fleet modernisation has involved increasing standardisation on low-floor Dennis Darts with Wright bodywork, of which twelve are now held. P667PNM stands at Watford Junction in April 1997. *Tony Wilson*

FLEET LISTS

Standard body codes are used in the following fleet lists, showing the body type, seating capacity and entrance position in that order.

Body Type		
	Single-deck bus	B
	Single-deck coach	C
	Dual-purpose vehicle	DP
	Dual-purpose double-deck vehicle	DPH
	Highbridge double-deck bus	H

Seating capacity For double-deckers the upper-deck capacity is shown first, followed by that for the lower deck. Standee capacities have not been shown as there are sometimes local variations between the licensed capacity of a vehicle and the operational capacity agreed with road staff.

Entrance position		
	Separate entrance and exit (front and centre) with doors	D
	Front entrance with platform doors	F
	Rear entrance without doors	R
	Rear entrance with platform doors	RD

The further suffix 'L' indicates a vehicle fitted with a wheelchair tail-lift. 'T' indicates a vehicle which contains a toilet compartment.

Fleet number suffixes		
	Vehicle restricted to staff bus duties	s
	Vehicle restricted to training work	t
	Vehicle unlicensed long-term	u
	Vehicle withdrawn for disposal	w

ARRIVA HERTS & ESSEX (COUNTY BUS)

BD357t	OJN357P	Bedford YRT	Duple	C32F	1976	Ex Welwyn-Hatfield Line, 1990
BOV594	HDZ8354	Bova FHD12.280	Bova Futura	C49F	1986	Ex Smith, Birmingham, 1995
BOV595	G545JOG	Bova FHD12.290	Bova Futura	C46F	1990	Ex Smith, Birmingham, 1995
BOV596	JIW3696	Bova FHD12.280	Bova Futura	C47F	1988	Ex Smith, Birmingham, 1994
BP504t	DDX741T	Bedford YLQ	Plaxton	C45F	1978	Ex Davian, Enfield, 1991
BP507t	SGS497W	Bedford YMT	Plaxton	C53F	1981	Ex Davian, Enfield, 1991
DI4	P754RWU	DAF DE33WSSB3000	Ikarus 350	C53F	1997	Ex Leaside, 1997
DIB56	J56GCX	DAF SB220LC550	Ikarus	B48F	1992	Ex South London, 1997
DIB124	K124TCP	DAF SB220LC550	Ikarus	B48F	1992	Ex South London, 1997
DIB926	J926CYL	DAF SB220LC550	Ikarus	B48F	1992	Ex Grey-Green, 1997
DIB927	J927CYL	DAF SB220LC550	Ikarus	B48F	1992	Ex Grey-Green, 1997
DIB928	J928CYL	DAF SB220LC550	Ikarus	B48F	1992	Ex Grey-Green, 1997
DP1	N551LUA	DAF DE33WSSB3000	Plaxton Première 350	C49F	1996	Ex Leaside, 1997
DP2	N552LUA	DAF DE33WSSB3000	Plaxton Première 350	C49F	1996	Ex Leaside, 1997
DP3	P753RWU	DAF DE33WSSB3000	Plaxton Première 350	C53F	1997	Ex Leaside, 1997

DP301-313		Dennis Dart 9SDL3002*	Plaxton Pointer	B35F	1991	* 302-7/13 are 9SDL3011; 309 rebodied 1992

301	J301WHJ	303	J303WHJ	305	J305WHJ	307	J307WHJ	309	J309WHJ	311	J311WHJ	313	J313WHJ
302	J302WHJ	304	J304WHJ	306	J306WHJ	308	J308WHJ	310	J310WHJ	312	J312WHJ		

DP318	K318CVX	Dennis Dart 9SDL3011	Plaxton Pointer	B35F	1992
DP319	K319CVX	Dennis Dart 9SDL3011	Plaxton Pointer	B35F	1992
DP320	K320CVX	Dennis Dart 9SDL3011	Plaxton Pointer	B35F	1992
DP321	K321CVX	Dennis Dart 9SDL3011	Plaxton Pointer	B35F	1992
DP322	K322CVX	Dennis Dart 9SDL3011	Plaxton Pointer	B35F	1992
DP323	K323CVX	Dennis Dart 9SDL3011	Plaxton Pointer	B35F	1992

DP324-334		Dennis Dart SFD212BR5	Plaxton Pointer	B34F	1996

DP324	P324HVX	DP326	P326HVX	DP328	P328HVX	DP330	P330HVX	DP332	P332HVX	DP334	P334HVX
DP325	P325HVX	DP327	P327HVX	DP329	P329HVX	DP331	P331HVX	DP333	P833HVX	

DP545	K545ORH	Dennis Dart 9SDL3016	Plaxton Pointer	B34F	1992	Ex Leaside, 1996
DP546	K546ORH	Dennis Dart 9SDL3016	Plaxton Pointer	B34F	1992	Ex Leaside, 1996
DP951	M951LYR	Dennis Dart 9.8SDL3040	Plaxton Pointer	B40F	1995	Ex Grey-Green, 1996

DPL405-414		Dennis Dart 9.8SDL3018	Plaxton Pointer	B40F	1993

405	K405FHJ	407	K407FHJ	409	K409FHJ	411	K411FHJ	413	K413FHJ
406	K406FHJ	408	K408FHJ	410	K410FHJ	412	K412FHJ	414	K414FHJ

DPP416-431			Dennis Dart SFD212BR1		Plaxton Pointer				B36F		1997

416	R416COO	419	R419COO	422	R422COO	425	R425COO	428	R428COO	431	R431COO
417	R417COO	420	R420COO	423	R423COO	426	R426COO	429	R429COO		
418	R418COO	421	R421COO	424	R424COO	427	R427COO	430	R430COO		

DW64	J64BJN	Dennis Dart 9.8SDL3012	Wright Handybus	DP40F	1992	Ex West, Woodford Green, 1997
DW65	J65BJN	Dennis Dart 9SDL3011	Wright Handybus	B35F	1992	Ex West, Woodford Green, 1997
DW314	J314XVX	Dennis Dart 9SDL3011	Wright Handybus	B35F	1992	
DW315	J315XVX	Dennis Dart 9SDL3011	Wright Handybus	B35F	1992	
DW316	J316XVX	Dennis Dart 9SDL3011	Wright Handybus	B35F	1992	
DW317	J317XVX	Dennis Dart 9SDL3011	Wright Handybus	B35F	1992	
DW761	K761JVX	Dennis Dart 9.8SDL3017	Wright Handybus	B40F	1992	Ex West, Woodford Green, 1997
DW762	K762JVX	Dennis Dart 9.8SDL3017	Wright Handybus	B40F	1992	Ex West, Woodford Green, 1997
DWL401	J401XVX	Dennis Dart 9.8SDL3012	Wright Handybus	B40F	1992	
DWL402	J402XVX	Dennis Dart 9.8SDL3012	Wright Handybus	B40F	1992	
DWL403	J403XVX	Dennis Dart 9.8SDL3012	Wright Handybus	B40F	1992	
DWL404	J404XVX	Dennis Dart 9.8SDL3012	Wright Handybus	B40F	1992	
DWL415	L415NHJ	Dennis Dart 9.8SDL3025	Wright Handybus	B40F	1994	
ELW266	M266VPU	Dennis Lance SLF 11SDA3201	Wright Pathfinder 320	B40F	1994	
ELW267	M267VPU	Dennis Lance SLF 11SDA3201	Wright Pathfinder 320	B40F	1994	
ELW268	M268VPU	Dennis Lance SLF 11SDA3201	Wright Pathfinder 320	B40F	1994	
ELW269	M269VPU	Dennis Lance SLF 11SDA3201	Wright Pathfinder 320	B40F	1994	
LP5u	FYT335V	Leyland Leopard PSU3E/4R	Plaxton Supreme IV Express	C49F	1979	Ex Cowie Leaside, 1996
LP6u	FYT336V	Leyland Leopard PSU3E/4R	Plaxton Supreme IV Express	C49F	1979	Ex Cowie Leaside, 1996

LR1-23			Leyland Olympian ONTL11/1R		Roe				H43/29F		1982	Ex London Country North East, 1989

1	TPD101X	3u	TPD103X	5u	TPD105X	9	TPD109X	11u	TPD111X	17	TPD117X
2	TPD102X	4	TPD104X	7	TPD107X	10	TPD110X	15	TPD115X	23	TPD123X

LX251-258			Leyland Lynx LX2R11C15Z4S		Leyland			B49F		1990

LX251	H251GEV	LX253	H253GEV	LX255	H255GEV	LX257	H257GEV
LX252	H252GEV	LX254	H254GEV	LX256	H256GEV	LX258	H258GEV

LX888	E888KYW	Leyland Lynx LX1126LXCTZR1	Leyland	B47F	1987	Ex Grey-Green, 1996
LX889	E889KYW	Leyland Lynx LX1126LXCTZR1	Leyland	B47F	1987	Ex Grey-Green, 1996
M1	GBU1V	MCW Metrobus DR101/6	MCW	H43/30F	1979	Ex Leaside, 1997
M4	GBU4V	MCW Metrobus DR101/6	MCW	H43/30F	1979	Ex Leaside, 1997
M5	GBU5V	MCW Metrobus DR101/6	MCW	H43/30F	1979	Ex Leaside, 1997
M8	GBU8V	MCW Metrobus DR101/6	MCW	H43/30F	1979	Ex Leaside, 1997
M9	GBU9V	MCW Metrobus DR101/6	MCW	H43/30F	1979	Ex Leaside, 1997
M80	JBO80W	MCW Metrobus DR102/20	MCW	H46/31F	1981	Ex Newport, 1994
M170	BYX170V	MCW Metrobus DR101/9	MCW	H43/28D	1979	Ex Leaside, 1997
M175	BYX175V	MCW Metrobus DR101/9	MCW	H43/28D	1979	Ex Leaside, 1997

M366	DTG366V	MCW Metrobus DR101/15		MCW				H46/31F	1980	Ex Grey-Green, 1997		
M367	DTG367V	MCW Metrobus DR101/15		MCW				H46/31F	1980	Ex Grey-Green, 1997		
M372	DTG372V	MCW Metrobus DR101/15		MCW				H46/31F	1980	Ex Grey-Green, 1997		
M537	GYE537W	MCW Metrobus DR101/14		MCW				H43/28D	1981	Ex Leaside, 1997		
M573	GYE573W	MCW Metrobus DR101/14		MCW				H43/28D	1981	Ex Leaside, 1997		
M625	KYO625X	MCW Metrobus DR101/14		MCW				H43/28D	1981	Ex Leaside, 1997		
M649	KYV649X	MCW Metrobus DR101/14		MCW				H43/28D	1981	Ex Leaside, 1997		
M1248	B248WUL	MCW Metrobus DR101/17		MCW				H43/28D	1985	Ex Leaside, 1997		
M1367	C367BUV	MCW Metrobus DR101/17		MCW				DPH43/28D	1985	Ex Leaside, 1997		
M1379	VLT88	MCW Metrobus DR101/17		MCW				DPH43/28F	1985	Ex Leaside, 1997		
M1398	C398BUV	MCW Metrobus DR101/17		MCW				H43/28D	1985	Ex Leaside, 1997		
M1437	VLT12	MCW Metrobus DR101/17		MCW				DPH43/24F	1986	Ex Leaside, 1997		
MB45	D45OKH	Iveco Daily 49.10		Robin Hood City Nippy				DP19F	1987	Ex London Country North East, 1989		
MB52	E352NEG	Iveco Daily 49.10		Robin Hood City Nippy				DP19F	1988	Ex London Country North East, 1989		
MB53	E353NEG	Iveco Daily 49.10		Robin Hood City Nippy				DP19F	1988	Ex London Country North East, 1989		
MB54	E354NEG	Iveco Daily 49.10		Robin Hood City Nippy				DP19F	1988	Ex London Country North East, 1989		
MB115	F115JGS	Iveco Daily 49.10		Robin Hood City Nippy				B25F	1988	Ex Sampsons, Hoddesdon, 1989		
MB154	F154DKU	Iveco Daily 49.10		Reeve Burgess Beaver				DP25F	1988	Ex demonstrator, 1989		
MB706	E296VOM	Iveco Daily 49.10		Carlyle Dailybus 2				B23F	1988	Ex Southend, 1992		
MB707	K707FNO	Iveco Turbo Daily 59.12		Dormobile Routemaker				B25F	1993			
MB708	K708FNO	Iveco Turbo Daily 59.12		Dormobile Routemaker				B25F	1993			
MB709	K709FNO	Iveco Turbo Daily 59.12		Dormobile Routemaker				B25F	1993			
MB710	K710FNO	Iveco Turbo Daily 59.12		Dormobile Routemaker				B25F	1993			
MB711	K711FNO	Iveco Turbo Daily 59.12		Dormobile Routemaker				B25F	1993			
MB712	K712FNO	Iveco Turbo Daily 59.12		Dormobile Routemaker				B25F	1993			

MB717-744		Iveco Turbo Daily 59.12		Marshall C31				B25F	1994/5			
717	L717OVX	721	M721UTW	725	M725UTW	729	M729UTW	733	M733AOO	737	M737AOO	741	N741AVW
718	L718OVX	722	L722OVX	726	M726UTW	730	M730AOO	734	M734AOO	738	M738AOO	742	N742AVW
719	M719UTW	723	L723PHK	727	M727UTW	731	M731AOO	735	M735AOO	739	N739AVW	743	N743AVW
720	M720UTW	724	L724PHK	728	M728UTW	732	M732AOO	736	M736AOO	740	N740AVW	744	N744AVW

MB748	E448TYG	Iveco Daily 49.10		Robin Hood City Nippy				DP25F	1988	Ex Keighley & District, 1993		
MB795	F795JKX	Iveco Daily 49.10		Reeve Burgess Beaver				B21F	1988	Ex Welwyn & Hatfield, 1992		
MB796	F796JKX	Iveco Daily 49.10		Reeve Burgess Beaver				B21F	1988	Ex Welwyn & Hatfield, 1992		

MB918-938		Mercedes-Benz 709D		Reeve Burgess Beaver*				B23F	1989-92	* MB933-8 are Plaxton Beaver		
918	G918UPP	925	G925WGS	928	G928WGS	931	G931WGS	934	J934WHJ	937	J937WHJ		
919	G919UPP	926	G926WGS	929	G929WGS	932	G932WGS	935	J935WHJ	938	J938WHJ		
924	G924WGS	927	G927WGS	930	G930WGS	933	J933WHJ	936	J936WHJ				

MB939	P939HVX	Mercedes-Benz 711D		Plaxton Beaver				DP25F	1997			

MB940-954 — Mercedes-Benz O814D — Plaxton Beaver 2 — B27F — 1998 — On order

940	R940VPU	943	R943VPU	946	R946VPU	949	R949VPU	952	R952VPU
941	R941VPU	944	R944VPU	947	R947VPU	950	R950VPU	953	R953VPU
942	R942VPU	945	R945VPU	948	R948VPU	951	R951VPU	954	R954VPU

MBT713	L713OVX	Iveco Turbo Daily 59.12	Marshall C31C	B18FL	1994
MBT714	L714OVX	Iveco Turbo Daily 59.12	Marshall C31C	B18FL	1994
MBT715	L715OVX	Iveco Turbo Daily 59.12	Marshall C31C	B18FL	1994
MBT716	L716OVX	Iveco Turbo Daily 59.12	Marshall C31C	B18FL	1994
MBT801	L801KNO	Peugeot-Talbot Freeway	TBP	B18FL	1993
MBT802	L802KNO	Peugeot-Talbot Freeway	TBP	B18FL	1993
MBT803	L803KNO	Peugeot-Talbot Freeway	TBP	B18FL	1993
MBT804	L804KNO	Peugeot-Talbot Freeway	TBP	B18FL	1993
MBT805	L805OVX	Peugeot-Talbot Freeway	TBP	B18FL	1994
MBT865	P865VTJ	LDV Convoy	Whitacres	B8FL	1997
MC540	D40MAG	Iveco Daily 49.10	Robin Hood City Nippy	C16F	1987	Ex West Yorkshire Road Car, 1989

MD601-612 — Mercedes-Benz 811D — Reeve Burgess Beaver — B28F — 1991

601	J601WHJ	603	J603WHJ	605	J605WHJ	607	J607WHJ	609	J609WHJ	611	J611WHJ
602	J602WHJ	604	J604WHJ	606	J606WHJ	608	J608WHJ	610	J610WHJ	612	J612WHJ

MD613	L613LVX	Mercedes-Benz 811D	Dormobile Routemaker	B31F	1993	
MD614	L614LVX	Mercedes-Benz 811D	Dormobile Routemaker	B31F	1993	
MR367	F367CHE	MCW Metrorider MF150/110	MCW	B23F	1988	Ex West, Woodford Green, 1997
MR667	E667YDT	MCW Metrorider MF150/65	MCW	B23F	1988	Ex West, Woodford Green, 1997
MR713	F713CWJ	MCW Metrorider MF150/110	MCW	B23F	1988	Ex West, Woodford Green, 1997
MR714	F714CWJ	MCW Metrorider MF150/110	MCW	B23F	1988	Ex West, Woodford Green, 1997
MR715	F715CWJ	MCW Metrorider MF150/110	MCW	B23F	1988	Ex West, Woodford Green, 1997
MR718	F718CWJ	MCW Metrorider MF150/110	MCW	B23F	1988	Ex West, Woodford Green, 1997
MR719	F719CWJ	MCW Metrorider MF150/110	MCW	B23F	1988	Ex West, Woodford Green, 1997
OD621	G621YMG	DAF SB220LC550	Optare Delta	B47F	1989	Ex West, Woodford Green, 1997
OD760	K760JVX	DAF SB220LC550	Optare Delta	B49F	1992	Ex West, Woodford Green, 1997

PDL201-209 — DAF DE02GGSB220 — Plaxton Prestige — DP37F — 1997

201	R201VPU	203	R203VPU	205	R205VPU	207	R207VPU	209	R209VPU
202	R202VPU	204	R204VPU	206	R206VPU	208	R208VPU		

RMC1453	453CLT	AEC Routemaster 6RM	Park Royal	H32/25RD	1962	Ex Leaside, 1997
RMC1464	464CLT	AEC Routemaster 6RM	Park Royal	O36/25RD	1962	Ex Leaside, 1997
RV1	GJG750D	AEC Regent V 2D3RA	Park Royal	H40/32F	1966	Ex Leaside, 1997
SLF165	R165GNW	Dennis Dart SFD212BR1	Wright	B36F	1997	
SLF169	R169GNW	Dennis Dart SFD212BR1	Wright	B41F	1997	
SLF170	R170GNW	Dennis Dart SFD212BR1	Wright	B41F	1997	
SLF416	P416HVX	Dennis Dart SFD322BR1	Wright Crusader	B41F	1996	
SLF417	P417HVX	Dennis Dart SFD322BR1	Wright Crusader	B41F	1996	

Fleet No.	Reg.	Chassis	Body	Seating	Year	Notes
SLF418	P418HVX	Dennis Dart SFD322BR1	Wright Crusader	B41F	1996	
SLF419-431		Dennis Dart SFD322BR1	Plaxton Pointer	B43F	1996	

419	P419HVX	**421**	P421HVX	**423**	P423HVX	**425**	P425HVX	**427**	P427HVX	**429**	P429HVX	**431**	P431HVX
420	P420HVX	**422**	P422HVX	**424**	P424HVX	**426**	P426HVX	**428**	P428HVX	**430**	P430HVX		

Fleet No.	Reg.	Chassis	Body	Seating	Year	Notes
STL10	BAZ7384	Leyland Tiger TRCTL11/3RH	Plaxton Paramount 3500 2	C49F	1985	Ex London & Country, 1992
T69	70CLT	Leyland Titan TNLXB2RRSp	Park Royal	O44/26D	1979	Ex Leaside, 1997
T83	CUL83V	Leyland Titan TNLXB2RRSp	Park Royal	O44/26D	1979	Ex Leaside, 1997
T100	CUL100V	Leyland Titan TNLXB2RRSp	Park Royal	O44/26D	1979	Ex Leaside, 1997
TDB61	F61FMC	Leyland Tiger TRBTL11/2RP	Duple 300	B55F	1988	Ex Sovereign, 1989
TDB62	F62FMC	Leyland Tiger TRBTL11/2RP	Duple 300	B55F	1988	Ex Sovereign, 1989
TDB63	F63FMC	Leyland Tiger TRBTL11/2RP	Duple 300	B55F	1988	Ex Sovereign, 1989
TDL54	C254SPC	Leyland Tiger TRCTL11/3RH	Duple 320	C53F	1986	Ex London & Country, 1993
TDL55	C255SPC	Leyland Tiger TRCTL11/3RH	Duple 320	C49F	1986	Ex London & Country, 1993
TDL60	C260SPC	Leyland Tiger TRCTL11/3RH	Duple 320	C49F	1986	Ex London & Country, 1993
TL13w	TPC113X	Leyland Tiger TRCTL11/2R	Eastern Coach Works B51	C49F	1982	Ex Copping & Wall, Stevenage, 1991
TL30t	WPH130Y	Leyland Tiger TRCTL11/2R	Eastern Coach Works B51	C49F	1982	Ex Luton & District, 1991
TPL1	124CLT	Leyland Tiger TRCTL11/3ARZM	Plaxton Paramount 3200 3	C53F	1989	Ex Leaside, 1997
TPL2	361CLT	Leyland Tiger TRCTL11/3ARZM	Plaxton Paramount 3200 3	C53F	1989	Ex Leaside, 1997
TPL8	VLT18	Leyland Tiger TRCL10/3ARZA	Plaxton Paramount 3200 3	C53F	1991	Ex Leaside, 1997
TPL518	530MUY	Leyland Tiger TRCTL11/3ARZ	Plaxton Paramount 3500 3	C51F	1988	Ex Moore, Saffron Walden, 1993
VDL185	185CLT	Volvo B10M-61	Duple 320	C53F	1988	Ex Leaside, 1997
VDL205	205CLT	Volvo B10M-61	Duple 320	C53F	1988	Ex Leaside, 1997
VDL891	E891KYW	Volvo B10M-61	Duple 320	C53F	1988	Ex Grey-Green, 1996
VPB64	E564BNK	Volvo B10M-56	Plaxton Derwent II	B54F	1988	Ex Sampsons, Hoddesdon, 1989
VPB65	E565BNK	Volvo B10M-56	Plaxton Derwent II	B54F	1988	Ex Sampsons, Hoddesdon, 1989
VPL1	C874CYX	Volvo B10M-61	Plaxton	C53F	1986	Ex Leaside, 1997
VPL2	C876CYX	Volvo B10M-61	Plaxton	C53F	1986	Ex Leaside, 1997
VPL501	L501MOO	Volvo B10M-60	Plaxton Première 350	C49F	1993	
VPL503	H903AHS	Volvo B10M-60	Plaxton Paramount 3500 3	C53F	1991	Ex Park, Hamilton, 1994
WS350w	H350PNO	Leyland Swift LBM6T/2RA	Wadham Stringer	B39F	1991	Ex West, Woodford Green, 1997

Vehicle on loan

Fleet No.	Reg.	Chassis	Body	Seating	Year	Notes
M782	KYV782X	MCW Metrobus DR101/14	MCW	H43/28D	1982	On loan from Cowie Leaside

Previous registrations

BAZ7384	C210PPE	**J65BJN**	J6BUS	**70CLT**	CUL69V
FYT335V	JVF815V, 185CLT	**K760JVX**	K5BUS	**124CLT**	G661WMD
FYT336V	JVF816V, 205CLT	**K761JVX**	K2BUS	**185CLT**	E892KYW
G621YMG	G259FHD, A10BUS	**K762JVX**	J12BUS	**205CLT**	E893KYW
HDZ8354	C904JOF, 245DOC, C566LOG	**OJN357P**	MGS22P, 9424RU	**361CLT**	G662WMD
H350PNO	H550AMT, A19BUS, H20BUS	**VLT12**	C437BUV	**530MUY**	E118KFV
JIW3696	E908UOH	**VLT18**	H643GRO		
J64BJN	J9BUS	**VLT88**	C379BUV		

Special liveries

Allover advertisement: LR4/5/15, MB54/706/918/32, TL13
Green Line: PDL201-9, TDL54/5/60
Leaside Travel: BOV594-6, DI4, DP1-3, LP5/6, M170/5, M537/73, M625/49, M1248, M1367/79/98, M1437, STL10, TPL518, T69, T83, T100, TPL1/2/8, VDL891, VPL1/2, VPL501/3
LT Mobility Bus: MBT713-6
LT red: RMC1453/64, RV1
Red and cream (Hertford Road services): DIB56/124/926-8, LR7/10/3, M1/4/5/8/9
Sampson: MC540
WAGN Ware Rail Link: MB939
Wests: DW64/5, DW761/2, MR713, WS350

ARRIVA KENT THAMESIDE (KENTISH BUS)

AN210w	EPH210V	Leyland Atlantean AN68A/1R		Roe				H43/30F	1979	Ex London Country, 1986	
AN221w	EPH221V	Leyland Atlantean AN68A/1R		Roe				H43/30F	1980	Ex London Country, 1986	
AN276w	KPJ276W	Leyland Atlantean AN68A/1R		Roe				H43/30F	1981	Ex London Country, 1986	
618w	B248NVN	Leyland Olympian ONLXB/1R		Eastern Coach Works				H45/32F	1985	Ex Northumbria, 1991	
869w	F932LKE	MCW Metrorider MF154/13		MCW				B33F	1988	Ex Boro'line Maidstone, 1992	
1154	J154NKN	Mercedes-Benz 814D		Dormobile Routemaker				B33F	1992	Ex Crossways, Swanley, 1996	

1444-1453		Optare MetroRider MR17		Optare				B29F	1994	Ex Londonlinks, 1996/7	
1444	M444HPF	1446	M446HPF	1448	M448HPF	1450	M450HPF	1452	M452HPG		
1445	M445HPF	1447	M447HPF	1449	M449HPF	1451	M451HPF	1453	M453HPG		

1801-1808		Optare MetroRider MR15		Optare				B29F	1996		
1801	N801BKN	1803	N803BKN	1805	N805BKN	1807	N807BKN				
1802	N802BKN	1804	N804BKN	1806	N806BKN	1808	N808BKN				

1809	R809TKO	Optare MetroRider		Optare		B29F	1998	On order		
1810	R810TKO	Optare MetroRider		Optare		B29F	1998	On order		
1811	R811TKO	Optare MetroRider		Optare		B29F	1998	On order		
1812	R812TKO	Optare MetroRider		Optare		B29F	1998	On order		
1813	R813TKO	Optare MetroRider		Optare		B29F	1998	On order		
1814	R814TKO	Optare MetroRider		Optare		B29F	1998	On order		
1844	E34NEF	MCW Metrorider MF154/9		MCW		DP31F	1988	Ex Londonlinks, 1995		
1852	N852YKE	Optare MetroRider MR13		Optare		B25F	1995	Ex Londonlinks, 1996		
1862	F862LCU	MCW Metrorider MF158/15		MCW		B31F	1988	Ex Maidstone & District, 1997		
1863	F863LCU	MCW Metrorider MF158/15		MCW		B31F	1988	Ex Maidstone & District, 1997		
1864	F864LCU	MCW Metrorider MF158/15		MCW		B31F	1988	Ex Londonlinks, 1995		
1866	G866TCU	Optare MetroRider MR01		Optare		B31F	1989	Ex Londonlinks, 1995		
1886	H886CCU	Optare MetroRider		Optare		B25F	1991			

1887	H887CCU	Optare MetroRider	Optare	B25F	1991	
1889	H889CCU	Optare MetroRider	Optare	B25F	1991	
1890	H890CCU	Optare MetroRider	Optare	B25F	1991	
1961	J961JNL	Optare MetroRider	Optare	B25F	1991	
1962	J962JNL	Optare MetroRider	Optare	B25F	1991	
1970	J970JNL	Optare MetroRider	Optare	B25F	1991	
1973	J973JNL	Optare MetroRider	Optare	B25F	1991	
1974	J974JNL	Optare MetroRider	Optare	B25F	1991	
1975	J975JNL	Optare MetroRider	Optare	B25F	1991	
1977	L837MWT	Optare MetroRider MR01	Optare	B31F	1993	Ex Darlington, 1995
1978	L838MWT	Optare MetroRider MR01	Optare	B31F	1993	Ex Londonlinks, 1995
2209	TIB5905	Leyland Tiger TRCTL11/3RH	Duple 320	C53F	1986	Ex London Country, 1986
2830	TIB5903	Volvo B10M-61	Van Hool Alizée	C53F	1988	Ex Jason, St Mary Cray, 1993
2831	TIB5904	Volvo B10M-61	Van Hool Alizée	C53F	1988	Ex Jason, St Mary Cray, 1993
3053	H813EKJ	Leyland Lynx LX2R11G15Z4S	Leyland	B49F	1991	Ex Boro'line Maidstone, 1992
3054	H815EKJ	Leyland Lynx LX2R11G15Z4S	Leyland	B49F	1991	Ex Boro'line Maidstone, 1992

3056-3065		Leyland Lynx LX2R11C15Z4S	Leyland	B49F	1989	Ex Boro'line Maidstone, 1992
						(3065 ex Maidstone & District, 1997)

3056	G36VME	3058	G38VME	3060	G40VME	3062	G42VME	3064	G44VME
3057	G37VME	3059	G39VME	3061	G41VME	3063	G43VME	3065	G45VME

3087	G217LGK	Dennis Dart 9SDL3002	Duple/Carlyle Dartline	B36F	1990	Ex R&I Tours, London NW10, 1995
3093	G123RGT	Dennis Dart 9SDL3002	Duple/Carlyle Dartline	B36F	1990	Ex R&I Tours, London NW10, 1995
3095	G125RGT	Dennis Dart 9SDL3002	Duple/Carlyle Dartline	B36F	1990	Ex R&I Tours, London NW10, 1995
3096	G126RGT	Dennis Dart 9SDL3002	Duple/Carlyle Dartline	B36F	1990	Ex R&I Tours, London NW10, 1995
3097	G127RGT	Dennis Dart 9SDL3002	Duple/Carlyle Dartline	B36F	1990	Ex R&I Tours, London NW10, 1995
3098	G128RGT	Dennis Dart 9SDL3002	Duple/Carlyle Dartline	B36F	1990	Ex R&I Tours, London NW10, 1995

3112-3159		Dennis Dart 9SDL3034	Northern Counties Paladin	B35F	1994

3112	L112YVK	3129	L129YVK	3134	L134YVK	3139u	L139YVK	3144	L144YVK	3150	L150YVK	3157	L157YVK
3113	L113YVK	3130	L130YVK	3135	L135YVK	3140u	L140YVK	3145	L145YVK	3152	L152YVK	3158	L158BFT
3114	L114YVK	3131	L131YVK	3136	L136YVK	3141	L141YVK	3146	L146YVK	3153	L153YVK	3159	L159BFT
3127	L127YVK	3132	L132YVK	3137	L137YVK	3142	L142YVK	3148	L148YVK	3154	L154YVK		
3128	L128YVK	3133	L133YVK	3138	L138YVK	3143	L143YVK	3149	L149YVK	3155	L155YVK		

3184	P184LKL	Dennis Dart SFD212BR1	Plaxton Pointer	B37F	1996
3185	P185LKL	Dennis Dart SFD212BR1	Plaxton Pointer	B37F	1996
3186	P186LKJ	Dennis Dart SFD322BR1	Plaxton Pointer	B40F	1997
3187	P187LKJ	Dennis Dart SFD322BR1	Plaxton Pointer	B40F	1997
3188	P188LKJ	Dennis Dart SFD322BR1	Plaxton Pointer	B40F	1997
3189	P189LKJ	Dennis Dart SFD322BR1	Plaxton Pointer	B40F	1997
3190	P190LKJ	Dennis Dart SFD322BR1	Plaxton Pointer	B40F	1997
3191	P191LKJ	Dennis Dart SFD322BR1	Plaxton Pointer	B40F	1997

| 3250-3259 | | | Scania L113CRL | | | Wright Access Ultralow | | | B43F | 1995 | |

| 3250 | N250BKK | 3252 | N252BKK | 3254 | N254BKK | 3256 | N256BKK | 3258 | N258BKK |
| 3251 | N251BKK | 3253 | N253BKK | 3255 | N255BKK | 3257 | N257BKK | 3259 | N259BKK |

| 3261-3272 | | | Dennis Dart SLF | | | Plaxton Pointer | | | B—F | 1998 | On Order |

| 3261 | R261EKO | 3263 | R263EKO | 3265 | R265EKO | 3267 | R267EKO | 3269 | R269EKO | 3271 | R271EKO |
| 3262 | R262EKO | 3264 | R264EKO | 3266 | R266EKO | 3268 | R268EKO | 3270 | R270EKO | 3272 | R272EKO |

3335	SIB6705	Leyland National 10351A/1R	East Lancs (1992)	B41F	1978	Ex Londonlinks, 1996
3336	SIB6706	Leyland National 2 NL106AL11/1R	East Lancs (1992)	B41F	1981	Ex Londonlinks, 1996
3337	SIB6707	Leyland National 2 NL106AL11/1R	East Lancs (1992)	B41F	1981	Ex Londonlinks, 1996
3338	SIB6708	Leyland National 2 NL106AL11/1R	East Lancs (1992)	B41F	1982	Ex Londonlinks, 1996
3345	SIB6715	Leyland National 1051/1R/0402	East Lancs (1993)	B41F	1973	Ex Londonlinks, 1996
3346	SIB6716	Leyland National 1051/1R/0402	East Lancs (1993)	B41F	1974	Ex Londonlinks, 1996
3361	PDZ6261	Leyland National 10351/1R	East Lancs (1994)	B41F	1977	Ex Londonlinks, 1996
3362	PDZ6262	Leyland National 10351/1R	East Lancs (1994)	B41F	1977	Ex Londonlinks, 1996
3492	RUF42R	Leyland National 11351/2R		B25DL	1977	Ex London Buses, 1993
3493	THX202S	Leyland National 10351A/2R		B21DL	1978	Ex London Buses, 1993
3494	YYE290T	Leyland National 10351A/2R		B21DL	1979	Ex London Buses, 1993

| 5557-5565 | | | Volvo Olympian YN2RC16Z4 | | | Northern Counties Palatine 2 | | | H47/30F | 1994 | |

| 5557 | L557YCU | 5559 | L559YCU | 5562 | L562YCU | 5564 | L564YCU |
| 5558 | L558YCU | 5561 | L561YCU | 5563 | L563YCU | 5565 | L565YCU |

5601	WDC219Y	Leyland Olympian ONLXB/1R	Eastern Coach Works	H44/32F	1983	Ex Northumbria, 1991
5608	CEF231Y	Leyland Olympian ONLXB/1R	Eastern Coach Works	H45/32F	1983	Ex Northumbria, 1991
5616	B246NVN	Leyland Olympian ONLXB/1R	Eastern Coach Works	H45/32F	1985	Ex Northumbria, 1991
5619	B256RAJ	Leyland Olympian ONLXB/1R	Eastern Coach Works	H45/32F	1985	Ex Northumbria, 1990
5620	C257UAJ	Leyland Olympian ONLXB/1R	Eastern Coach Works	H45/32F	1985	Ex Northumbria, 1991

| 5751-5762 | | | Leyland Olympian ONLXB/1RH | | | Optare | | | H47/29F | 1988/89 | Ex Boro'line Maidstone, 1992 |

| 5751 | E151OMD | 5753 | E153OMD | 5755 | E155OMD | 5757 | E157OMD | 5759 | E159OMD | 5761 | E161OMD |
| 5752 | E152OMD | 5754 | E154OMD | 5756 | E156OMD | 5758 | E158OMD | 5760 | E160OMD | 5762 | F991UME |

5765	H765EKJ	Leyland Olympian ON2R50C13Z4	Northern Counties	H47/30F	1991	Ex Boro'line Maidstone, 1992
5766	H766EKJ	Leyland Olympian ON2R50C13Z4	Northern Counties	H47/30F	1991	Ex Boro'line Maidstone, 1992
5767	H767EKJ	Leyland Olympian ON2R50C13Z4	Northern Counties	H47/30F	1991	Ex Boro'line Maidstone, 1992
5768	H768EKJ	Leyland Olympian ON2R50C13Z4	Northern Counties	H47/30F	1991	Ex Boro'line Maidstone, 1992
5769	H769EKJ	Leyland Olympian ON2R50C13Z4	Northern Counties	H47/30F	1991	Ex Boro'line Maidstone, 1992
5770	H770EKJ	Leyland Olympian ON2R50C13Z4	Northern Counties	H47/30F	1991	Ex Boro'line Maidstone, 1992
6172	XPG172T	Leyland Atlantean AN68A/1R	Park Royal	H43/30F	1979	Ex Londonlinks, 1997
6186	XPG186T	Leyland Atlantean AN68A/1R	Roe	H43/30F	1979	Ex Londonlinks, 1996

6220-6282			Leyland Atlantean AN68A/1R			Roe				H43/30F		1979/81	Ex London Country, 1986		
6220	EPH220V	**6232**	EPH232V	**6270**	KPJ270W	**6271**	KPJ271W	**6274**	KPJ274W	**6277**	KPJ277W	**6282**	KPJ282W		

7631-7643			Volvo Citybus B10M-50			Northern Counties				H45/31F		1989	Ex Londonlinks, 1996/7		
7631	G631BPH	**7633**	G633BPH	**7635**	G635BPH	**7637**	G637BPH	**7639**	G639BPH	**7641**	G641BPH	**7643**	G643BPH
7632	G632BPH	**7634**	G634BPH	**7636**	G636BPH	**7638**	G638BPH	**7640**	G640BPH	**7642**	G642BPH		

7702	G641CHF	Volvo Citybus B10M-50	East Lancs	H49/39F	1989	Ex North Western, 1996
7703	G642CHF	Volvo Citybus B10M-50	East Lancs	H49/39F	1989	Ex North Western, 1996
7706	G648EKA	Volvo Citybus B10M-50	East Lancs	H49/39F	1990	Ex North Western, 1996
7707	G649EKA	Volvo Citybus B10M-50	East Lancs	H49/39F	1990	Ex North Western, 1996
7708	G659DTJ	Volvo Citybus B10M-50	East Lancs	H49/39F	1990	Ex North Western, 1996
7709	G660DTJ	Volvo Citybus B10M-50	East Lancs	H49/39F	1990	Ex North Western, 1996
7722	F102TML	Volvo Citybus B10M-50	Alexander RV	H47/29D	1989	Ex Londonlinks, 1997
7731	F111TML	Volvo Citybus B10M-50	Alexander RV	H47/29D	1989	Ex Londonlinks, 1997
7734	F114TML	Volvo Citybus B10M-50	Alexander RV	H47/29D	1989	Ex Boro'line Maidstone, 1992
7764	E164OMD	Volvo Citybus B10M-61	Alexander RV	H47/37F	1988	Ex Boro'line Maidstone, 1992

Previous registrations

F932LKE	F241JWV, 217UKL	**SIB6706**	LFR855X	**SIB6716**	UPE196M
PDZ6261	UPB310S	**SIB6707**	JCK850W	**TIB5903**	E316OPR
PDZ6262	UPB313S	**SIB6708**	LFR874X	**TIB5904**	E319OPR
SIB6705	YPF762T	**SIB6715**	TPD176M	**TIB5905**	C261SPC

Special liveries

Allover advertisements: 6274.
Green Line: 2209/830/1.
Green Traveller: 1978.
LT Mobility Bus: 3492-4.
Maroon and primrose: 1844/64/6/86/7/9/90, 1970/3/5, 3112-4/27-46/8-50/2-5/7-9, 5557-9/61-5, 5619, 5751-5/7-62/7/9/70, 6220, 7734/64.

ARRIVA SURREY & WEST SUSSEX (LONDON & COUNTRY)

AD1-10		Dennis Arrow		East Lancs				H45/35F*	1996	* AD9/10 are DPH45/31F
1	N801TPK	3	N803TPK	5	N805TPK	7	N807TPK	9	N809TPK	
2	N802TPK	4	N804TPK	6	N806TPK	8	N808TPK	10	N810TPK	

AN135-182		Leyland Atlantean AN68A/1R		Park Royal				H43/30F	1978/79	Ex London Country Bus Services, 1986
135	UPK135S	147	UPK147S	149	VPA149S	152	VPA152S	175	XPG175T	
146	UPK146S	148	VPA148S	151	VPA151S	153	VPA153S	182	XPG182T	

AN184	XPG184T	Leyland Atlantean AN68A/1R	Roe	H43/30F	1979	Ex London Country Bus Services, 1986
AN187	XPG187T	Leyland Atlantean AN68A/1R	Roe	H43/30F	1979	Ex London Country Bus Services, 1986
AN201	XPG201T	Leyland Atlantean AN68A/1R	Roe	H43/30F	1979	Ex London Country Bus Services, 1986
AN223	EPH223V	Leyland Atlantean AN68A/1R	Roe	H43/30F	1980	Ex London Country Bus Services, 1986
AN228	EPH228V	Leyland Atlantean AN68A/1R	Roe	H43/30F	1980	Ex London Country Bus Services, 1986
AN229	EPH229V	Leyland Atlantean AN68A/1R	Roe	H43/30F	1980	Ex London Country Bus Services, 1986

AN258-288		Leyland Atlantean AN68B/1R		Roe				H43/30F	1980/81	Ex London Country Bus Services, 1986
258	KPJ258W	267	KPJ267W	283	KPJ283W	285	KPJ285W	288	KPJ288W	
259	KPJ259W	281	KPJ281W	284	KPJ284W	286	KPJ286W			

BS407t	YPH407T	Bedford YMT	Plaxton Supreme IV	C53F	1978	Ex Blue Saloon, Guildford, 1996
BS820t	YPB820T	Bedford YMT	Plaxton Supreme IV	C53F	1978	Ex Blue Saloon, Guildford, 1996
BTL44	C144SPB	Leyland Tiger TRCTL11/3RH	Berkhof	C53F	1986	Ex London Country Bus Services, 1986
DD1	F201OPD	Dennis Dominator DDA1020	East Lancs	H51/33F	1988	

DD2-8		Dennis Dominator DDA1026		East Lancs				H45/31F	1989			
2	F602RPG	3	F603RPG	4	F604RPG	5	F605RPG	6	F606RPG	7	F607RPG	8	F608RPG

DD9	F609RPG	Dennis Dominator DDA1017	East Lancs	H49/35F	1989	
DD10	K36XNE	Dennis Dominator DDA2005	East Lancs	H45/31F	1993	Ex Mayne, Clayton, 1995
DD11	K37XNE	Dennis Dominator DDA2005	East Lancs	H45/31F	1993	Ex Mayne, Clayton, 1995
DD12	K38YVW	Dennis Dominator DDA2005	East Lancs	H45/31F	1993	Ex Mayne, Clayton, 1995
DD13	N713TPK	Dennis Dominator DDA2006	East Lancs	H45/31F	1996	
DD14	N714TPK	Dennis Dominator DDA2006	East Lancs	H45/31F	1996	
DD15	N715TPK	Dennis Dominator DDA2006	East Lancs	H45/31F	1996	
DD16	N716TPK	Dennis Dominator DDA2006	East Lancs	H45/31F	1996	
DD17u	G626EKA	Dennis Dominator DDA1031	East Lancs	H47/29F	1990	Ex North Western, 1997
DD18	G628EKA	Dennis Dominator DDA1031	East Lancs	H47/29F	1990	Ex North Western, 1997
DD19	F631BKD	Dennis Dominator DDA1026	East Lancs	DPH43/25F	1989	Ex North Western, 1997
DD20u	G663FKA	Dennis Dominator DDA1031	East Lancs	H47/29F	1990	Ex North Western, 1997
DD21u	G664FKA	Dennis Dominator DDA1031	East Lancs	H47/29F	1990	Ex North Western, 1997
DD22u	G665FKA	Dennis Dominator DDA1031	East Lancs	H47/29F	1990	Ex North Western, 1997
DFC1	OYJ693	DAF MB230LT615	Van Hool Alizée	C53FT	1989	Ex London Coaches, 1997

DFC2	F619HGO	DAF MB230LB615	Van Hool Alizée	C53FT	1989	Ex London Coaches, 1997
DFC3	G974KJX	DAF MB230LB615	Van Hool Alizée	C53FT	1990	Ex London Coaches, 1997
DFC4	J16AMB	DAF SB3000DKVF601	Van Hool Alizée	C46FT	1992	Ex Kentish Bus, 1997

DFD1-13 DAF DB250 Northern Counties Palatine H— 1998 On Order

1	R201CKO	3	R203CKO	5	R205CKO	7	R207CKO	9	R209CKO	11	R211CKO	13	R213CKO
2	R202CKO	4	R204CKO	6	R206CKO	8	R208CKO	10	R210CKO	12	R212CKO		

DS1-9 Dennis Dart 9.8SDL3035 East Lancs B40F 1993/94

1	L503CPB	3	L505CPJ	5	L507CPJ	7	L509CPJ	9	L511CPJ
2	L504CPB	4	L506CPJ	6	L508CPJ	8	L510CPJ		

DS10	M521HPF	Dennis Dart 9SDL3053	East Lancs EL2000	B30FL	1995
DS11	M522HPF	Dennis Dart 9SDL3053	East Lancs EL2000	B30FL	1995
DS12	M523HPF	Dennis Dart 9SDL3053	East Lancs EL2000	B30FL	1995
DS13	M524HPF	Dennis Dart 9SDL3053	East Lancs EL2000	B30FL	1995
DS14	M525MPM	Dennis Dart 9.8SDL3054	East Lancs EL2000	B40F	1995
DS15	M526MPM	Dennis Dart 9.8SDL3054	East Lancs EL2000	B40F	1995
DS16	N528SPA	Dennis Dart 9SDL3053	East Lancs EL2000	B30FL	1995
DS17	N529SPA	Dennis Dart 9SDL3053	East Lancs EL2000	B30FL	1995
DS18	N530SPA	Dennis Dart 9SDL3053	East Lancs EL2000	B30FL	1995
DS19	N539TPF	Dennis Dart 9.8SDL3054	East Lancs EL2000	B40F	1995
DS20	N540TPF	Dennis Dart 9.8SDL3054	East Lancs EL2000	B40F	1995
DS21	N541TPF	Dennis Dart 9.8SDL3054	East Lancs EL2000	B40F	1995
DS22	N542TPF	Dennis Dart 9.8SDL3054	East Lancs EL2000	B40F	1996
DS23	N543TPF	Dennis Dart 9.8SDL3054	East Lancs EL2000	B40F	1996
DS24	N544TPF	Dennis Dart 9.8SDL3054	East Lancs EL2000	B40F	1996

DSL25-36 Dennis Dart SFD212 Plaxton Pointer B35F 1996 On loan to London Buslines

25	N225TPK	27	N227TPK	29	N229TPK	31	N231TPK	33	N233TPK	35	N235TPK
26	N226TPK	28	N228TPK	30	N230TPK	32	N232TPK	34	N234TPK	36	N236TPK

DSL37-55 Dennis Dart SFD112 East Lancs Spryte B31F 1996

37	N237VPH	40	N240VPH	43	N243VPH	46	N246VPH	49	N249VPH	52	P252APM	55	P255APM
38	N238VPH	41	N241VPH	44	N244VPH	47	N247VPH	50	P250APM	53	P253APM		
39	N239VPH	42	N242VPH	45	N245VPH	48	N248VPH	51	P251APM	54	P254APM		

DSL68-108 Dennis Dart SFD322 Plaxton Pointer B39F 1997

68	P268FPK	74	P274FPK	80	P280FPK	86	P286FPK	92	P292FPK	98	R298CMV	104	R304CMV
69	P269FPK	75	P275FPK	81	P281FPK	87	P287FPK	93	P293FPK	99	R299CMV	105	R305CMV
70	P270FPK	76	P276FPK	82	P282FPK	88	P288FPK	94	P294FPK	100	R310CMV	106	R296CMV
71	P271FPK	77	P277FPK	83	P283FPK	89	P289FPK	95	P295FPK	101	R301CMV	107	R307CMV
72	P272FPK	78	P278FPK	84	P284FPK	90	P290FPK	96	P296FPK	102	R302CMV	108	R308CMV
73	P273FPK	79	P279FPK	85	P285FPK	91	P291FPK	97	R297CMV	103	R303CMV		

DT9t	SFD132R	Bristol LH6L	Eastern Coach Works	C41F	1977	
GF58	UFG58S	Leyland National 11351A/2R		B49F	1977	Ex Panther, Crawley, 1991
GF60	UFG60S	Leyland National 11351A/2R		B49F	1977	Ex Panther, Crawley, 1991
GF180	THX180S	Leyland National 10351A/2R		B41F	1978	Ex Panther, Crawley, 1991
GF313w	AYR313T	Leyland National 10351A/2R		B41F	1979	Ex Panther, Crawley, 1991
GS13	MXX313	Guy Special NLLVP	Eastern Coach Works	B26F	1953	Ex Sussex Bus, Ford, 1992
LNB28	JOX528P	Leyland National 11351A/1R		B25FL	1976	Ex Shamrock & Rambler, 1989
LNB36	NOE536R	Leyland National 11351A/1R		B49F	1976	Ex Midland Red (North), 1990
LNB546w	PKP546R	Leyland National 11351A/1R		B49F	1976	Ex Maidstone & District, 1995
LNB553	MEL553P	Leyland National 11351/1R		B49F	1976	Ex Hampshire Bus, 1993
LNB600	NOE600R	Leyland National 11351A/1R	(Urban bus)	B49F	1977	Ex Midland Red (North), 1994
LNC362	KDW362P	Leyland National 11351/1R/SC		DP48F	1975	Ex Rhondda, 1992

LR8-50		Leyland Olympian ONTL11/1R	Roe	H43/29F	1982/84	Ex London Country Bus Services, 1986

8	TPD108X	14	TPD114X	27	TPD127X	29	TPD129X	48	A148FPG
13	TPD113X	18	TPD118X	28	TPD128X	46	A146FPG	50	A150FPG

LR74	B274LPH	Leyland Olympian ONTL11/1R	Eastern Coach Works	H43/29F	1985	Ex London Country Bus Services, 1986
LR75	B275LPH	Leyland Olympian ONTL11/1R	Eastern Coach Works	H43/29F	1985	Ex London Country Bus Services, 1986
LR501	G501SFT	Leyland Olympian ONCL10/1RZ	Northern Counties	H47/30F	1989	Ex Kentish Bus, 1992
LR502	G502SFT	Leyland Olympian ONCL10/1RZ	Northern Counties	H47/30F	1989	Ex Kentish Bus, 1992
LR503	G503SFT	Leyland Olympian ONCL10/1RZ	Northern Counties	H47/30F	1989	Ex Kentish Bus, 1992
LR504	G504SFT	Leyland Olympian ONCL10/1RZ	Northern Counties	H47/30F	1989	Ex Kentish Bus, 1992

LS10-24		Dennis Lance 11SDA3113	East Lancs EL2000	B49F	1996	

10	N210TPK	13	N213TPK	16	N216TPK	19	N219TPK	22	N322TPK
11	N211TPK	14	N214TPK	17	N217TPK	20	N220TPK	23	N223TPK
12	N212TPK	15	N215TPK	18	N218TPK	21	N221TPK	24	N224TPK

LSL5	M517KPA	Dennis Lance SLF 11SDA3201	Wright Pathfinder	B40F	1995	
LSL6	M518KPA	Dennis Lance SLF 11SDA3201	Wright Pathfinder	B40F	1995	
LSL7	M519KPA	Dennis Lance SLF 11SDA3201	Wright Pathfinder	B40F	1995	
LSL8	M520KPA	Dennis Lance SLF 11SDA3201	Wright Pathfinder	B40F	1995	
LSL9	N527SPA	Dennis Lance SLF 11SDA3201	Wright Pathfinder	B40F	1995	
MBM468	N468SPA	Mercedes-Benz 709D	Alexander (Belfast) AM	B22FL	1995	
MBM469	N469SPA	Mercedes-Benz 709D	Alexander (Belfast) AM	B22FL	1995	
MBM470	N470SPA	Mercedes-Benz 709D	Alexander (Belfast) AM	B22FL	1995	
MM471	N671TPF	Mercedes-Benz 709D	Plaxton Beaver	B23F	1995	
MM473	P473APJ	Mercedes-Benz 711D	Plaxton Beaver	B27F	1996	
MM474	P474APJ	Mercedes-Benz 811D	Plaxton Beaver	B18FL	1996	
MM475	P475DPE	Mercedes-Benz 711D	Plaxton Beaver	B27F	1997	
MM476	P476DPE	Mercedes-Benz 711D	Plaxton Beaver	B27F	1997	
MM477	P477DPE	Mercedes-Benz 711D	Plaxton Beaver	B27F	1997	
MM479	P479DPE	Mercedes-Benz 711D	Plaxton Beaver	B27F	1997	

MM480	P480DPE	Mercedes-Benz 711D	Plaxton Beaver	B27F	1997	
MR472	P472APJ	Optare MetroRider	Optare	B29F	1996	
RMA16	KGJ614D	AEC Routemaster 9RM	Park Royal	H31/24F	1966	Ex preservation, 1996
RMC4	SLT59	AEC Routemaster 4RM	Eastern Coach Works	H32/25RD	1957	Ex London Country Bus Services, 1986; Leyland units
RP21w	JPA121K	AEC Reliance 6U2R	Park Royal	DP45F	1972	Ex AML, Hounslow, 1994
RT3775	NLE882	AEC Regent III 0961	Park Royal	H30/26R	1953	Ex preservation, 1994
SNB348	UPB348S	Leyland National 10351A/1R		B41F	1977	Ex London Country Bus Services, 1986
SNB349	UPB349S	Leyland National 10351A/1R		B41F	1977	Ex London Country Bus Services, 1986
SNB357	XPC17S	Leyland National 10351A/1R		B41F	1978	Ex London Country Bus Services, 1986

SNB376-394		Leyland National 10351B/1R	B41F	1978	Ex London Country Bus Services, 1986 (SNB394 ex Northumbria, 1994)

SNB376	YPL376T	**SNB378**	YPL378T	**SNB382**	YPL382T	**SNB393**	YPL393T
SNB377	YPL377T	**SNB380**	YPL380T	**SNB385**	YPL385T	**SNB394**	YPL394T

SNC420	YPL420T	Leyland National 10351B/1R	(Urban Bus)	B41F	1978	Ex London Country Bus Services, 1986

SNB427-543		Leyland National 10351B/1R	B41F	1978/79	Ex London Country Bus Services, 1986

SNB427	YPL427T	**SNB440**	YPL440T	**SNB459**	BPL459T	**SNB491**	BPL491T	**SNB511**	EPD511V	**SNB538**	EPD538V
SNB435w	YPL435T	**SNB450u**	YPL450T	**SNB475**	BPL475T	**SNB502u**	DPH502T	**SNB530**	EPD530V	**SNB543**	EPD543V

SR88	E88OJT	Leyland Tiger TRCTL11/3ARZA	Plaxton Paramount 3200 2	C53F	1988	Ex Shamrock & Rambler, 1989
SR89	E89OJT	Leyland Tiger TRCTL11/3ARZA	Plaxton Paramount 3200 2	C53F	1988	Ex Shamrock & Rambler, 1989
SR90	E90OJT	Leyland Tiger TRCTL11/3ARZA	Plaxton Paramount 3200 2	C53F	1988	Ex Shamrock & Rambler, 1989
TC426	HBH426Y	Leyland Tiger TRCTL11/3R	Plaxton Paramount 3200	C53F	1983	Ex Blue Saloon, Guildford, 1996
TDL46	C246SPC	Leyland Tiger TRCTL11/3RH	Duple 320	C53F	1986	
TDL66	ESK987	Leyland Tiger TRCTL11/3RH	Duple	C50F	1985	Ex Maidstone & District, 1997
TDL67	ESK988	Leyland Tiger TRCTL11/3RH	Duple	C50F	1985	Ex Maidstone & District, 1997
TP74	B274KPF	Leyland Tiger TRCTL11/2RH	Plaxton Paramount 3200 2 Exp	C49F	1985	
TP91	AEF990Y	Leyland Tiger TRCTL11/2R	Plaxton Paramount 3200 Exp	C53F	1983	
TPL44	A144EPA	Leyland Tiger TRCTL11/3R	Plaxton Paramount 3200 Exp	C51F	1984	Ex Southend, 1995
TPL54	A154EPA	Leyland Tiger TRCTL11/3R	Plaxton Paramount 3200 Exp	C57F	1984	
TPL85	B285KPF	Leyland Tiger TRCTL11/3RH	Plaxton Paramount 3200 2 Exp	C53F	1985	
TPL88	B288KPF	Leyland Tiger TRCTL11/3RH	Plaxton Paramount 3200 2 Exp	C53F	1985	
VCB89	C89NNV	Volvo B10M-61	Caetano Stagecoach	B57F	1986	Ex Tellings-Golden Miller, Byfleet, 1995

113	G113TND	Mercedes-Benz 811D	Carlyle	B33FL	1990	Ex Bee Line Buzz, 1992
132	K132XRE	Mercedes-Benz 709D	Dormobile Routemaker	B29F	1992	Ex Stevensons, Uttoxeter, 1994
133	J480XHL	Mercedes-Benz 709D	Alexander AM	DP25F	1991	Ex Stevensons, Uttoxeter, 1994
154	K154BRF	Mercedes-Benz 709D	Dormobile Routemaker	B29F	1993	Ex Stevensons, Uttoxeter, 1994
160t	CPG160T	AEC Reliance 6U3ZR	Plaxton	C53F	1979	
161	APM113T	AEC Reliance 6U2R	Plaxton Supreme IV Express	C53F	1979	Ex Eagle, Bristol, 1994
168	E168OMD	Volvo B10M-61	Plaxton Paramount 3200 3	C57F	1988	Ex Moon, Warnham, 1994

No.	Reg	Chassis	Body	Seating	Year	History
189	G689OHE	Mercedes-Benz 811D	Reeve Burgess Beaver	B20FL	1990	Ex Danks & Gaymer, Coseley, 1992
190	G690OHE	Mercedes-Benz 811D	Reeve Burgess Beaver	B20FL	1990	Ex Danks & Gaymer, Coseley, 1992
201	G101TND	Mercedes-Benz 814D	Carlyle	B31F	1989	Ex Bee Line Buzz, 1992
202	HPK504N	Leyland National 11351/1R	(Urban bus)	B49F	1975	Ex Alder Valley South, 1990
221	KPA372P	Leyland National 11351/1R		B49F	1975	Ex Alder Valley South, 1990
235w	KPA386P	Leyland National 11351A/1R		B49F	1976	Ex Alder Valley South, 1990
236u	M236KNR	Mercedes-Benz 709D	Alexander AM	B29F	1995	
242	LPF600P	Leyland National 11351/1R/SC		DP21FL	1976	Ex Alder Valley South, 1990
246	KPA367P	Leyland National 11351/1R		DP21FL	1975	Ex Alder Valley South, 1990
252	JCK852W	Leyland National 2 NL106AL11/1R	East Lancs (1991)	B40F	1981	Ex North Western, 1991
257	NPJ478R	Leyland National 11351A/1R		B49F	1976	Ex Alder Valley South, 1990
258w	NPJ479R	Leyland National 11351A/1R		B49F	1976	Ex Alder Valley South, 1990
265	PPM 892R	Leyland National 11351A/1R	(Urban bus)	B49F	1977	Ex Alder Valley South, 1990
270	BVP813V	Leyland National 2 NL116L11/1R		B49F	1980	Ex North Western, 1992
302	G302DPA	Dennis Falcon SDA421	East Lancs	B48F	1990	Ex Londonlinks, 1996
303	G303DPA	Dennis Falcon SDA421	East Lancs	B48F	1990	
304	G304DPA	Dennis Falcon SDA421	East Lancs	B48F	1990	
305	G305DPA	Dennis Falcon SDA421	East Lancs	B48F	1990	
339	SIB6709	Leyland National NL106AL11/1R	East Lancs (1992)	B41F	1982	Ex Londonlinks, 1996
341	SIB6711	Leyland National 10351/1R	East Lancs (1992)	B41F	1975	Ex Londonlinks, 1996
343	SIB6713	Leyland National 1051/1R	East Lancs (1992)	B41F	1974	Ex Londonlinks, 1996
344	SIB6714	Leyland National 10351/1R	East Lancs (1992)	B41F	1974	Ex Londonlinks, 1996
353	JIL2193	Leyland National 11351/1R	East Lancs (1994)	B49F	1974	Ex South Coast Buses, 1994
356	JIL2196	Leyland National 11351/1R	East Lancs (1994)	B49F	1975	Ex Westbus, Ashford, 1994
357	JIL2197	Leyland National 1151/1R/0102	East Lancs (1994)	B49F	1973	Ex Midland Fox, 1994
358	JIL2198	Leyland National 11351A/1R	East Lancs (1994)	B49F	1976	Ex Midland Fox, 1994
359	JIL2199	Leyland National 11351A/1R	East Lancs (1994)	B49F	1976	Ex Midland Fox, 1994
360	JIL2190	Leyland National 11351/1R	East Lancs (1994)	B49F	1976	Ex Midland Red (North), 1994
363	PDZ6263	Leyland National 11351A/1R	East Lancs (1994)	B49F	1977	Ex Tellings-Golden Miller, Byfleet, 1992
364	PDZ6264	Leyland National 11351A/1R	East Lancs (1994)	B49F	1979	Ex Tellings-Golden Miller, Byfleet, 1992
365	PDZ6265	Leyland National 11351/1R	East Lancs (1994)	B49F	1975	Ex Alder Valley South, 1990
366	SJI5066	Leyland National 11351A/1R	East Lancs (1994)	B49F	1977	Ex Tellings-Golden Miller, Byfleet, 1992
367	JIL5367	Leyland National 11351A/1R	East Lancs (1994)	B49F	1977	Ex Tellings-Golden Miller, Byfleet, 1992
368	IIL2168	Leyland National 11351A/1R	East Lancs (1994)	B49F	1977	Ex Tellings-Golden Miller, Byfleet, 1992
369	SJI5569	Leyland National 11351A/1R	East Lancs (1994)	B49F	1977	Ex The Bee Line, 1994
370	SJI5570	Leyland National 11351/1R	East Lancs (1994)	B49F	1976	Ex Midland Fox, 1994
371	SJI5571	Leyland National 11351A/1R	East Lancs (1994)	B49F	1976	Ex Midland Fox, 1994
372	SJI5572	Leyland National 11351/1R/SC	East Lancs (1994)	B49F	1976	Ex The Bee Line, 1994
373	PDZ6273	Leyland National 11351/1R	East Lancs (1994)	DP49F	1976	Ex Midland Fox, 1994
374	PDZ6274	Leyland National 11351A/1R	East Lancs (1994)	DP49F	1976	Ex Midland Fox, 1994
375	PDZ6275	Leyland National 11351A/2R	East Lancs (1994)	DP49F	1977	Ex Panther, Crawley, 1991
376	PDZ6276	Leyland National 11351/1R	East Lancs (1994)	DP49F	1975	Ex Northumbria, 1994
377	PDZ6277	Leyland National 11351A/1R	East Lancs (1994)	DP49F	1978	Ex Alder Valley South, 1990
378	RDZ4278	Leyland National 11351/1R	East Lancs (1995)	B49F	1975	Ex Shamrock & Rambler, 1988

379	RDZ4279	Leyland National 11351/1R		East Lancs (1995)				B49F	1975	Ex Alder Valley South, 1990				
380	LIL2180	Leyland National 11351/1R		East Lancs (1995)				B49F	1975	Ex Alder Valley South, 1990				
381	SIB1278	Leyland National 10351B/1R		East Lancs (1992)				B41F	1979	Ex Londonlinks, 1996				
402	K402VPK	Mercedes-Benz 709D		Dormobile				B25FL	1992					
403u	K403VPK	Mercedes-Benz 709D		Dormobile				B25FL	1992					
404u	K404VPK	Mercedes-Benz 709D		Dormobile				B25FL	1992					
405	K405VPK	Mercedes-Benz 709D		Dormobile				B25FL	1992					
422	L422CPB	Mercedes-Benz 709D		Dormobile				B25F	1993					
423	L423CPB	Mercedes-Benz 709D		Dormobile				B25F	1993					
424	L424CPB	Mercedes-Benz 709D		Dormobile				B25F	1993					
425	L425CPB	Mercedes-Benz 709D		Dormobile				B27F	1993					
426	L426CPB	Mercedes-Benz 709D		Dormobile				B27F	1993					
427	L427CPB	Mercedes-Benz 709D		Dormobile				B25F	1993					
428	L428CPC	Mercedes-Benz 709D		Danescroft				B27F	1993					
429	L429CPC	Mercedes-Benz 709D		Danescroft				B27F	1993					
438	L438FPA	Mercedes-Benz 709D		Plaxton Beaver				B23F	1994					
439	L439FPA	Mercedes-Benz 709D		Plaxton Beaver				B23F	1994					

454-460		Mercedes-Benz 709D		Alexander AM				B23F	1994					
454	M454HPG	**455**	M455HPG	**456**	M456HPG	**457**	M457HPG	**458**	M458JPA	**459**	M459JPA	**460**	M460JPA	

461	M461JPA	Mercedes-Benz 709D		Plaxton Beaver				B31F	1995					
462	M462JPA	Mercedes-Benz 709D		Plaxton Beaver				B31F	1995					
463	M463JPA	Mercedes-Benz 709D		Plaxton Beaver				B23F	1995					
464	M464JPA	Mercedes-Benz 709D		Plaxton Beaver				B23F	1995					
465	M465LPG	Mercedes-Benz 709D		Alexander (Belfast)				B29F	1995					
466	M466MPM	Mercedes-Benz 709D		Plaxton Beaver				B21F	1995					
467	M467MPM	Mercedes-Benz 709D		Plaxton Beaver				B21F	1995					
512	L512CPJ	Volvo B6-50		Plaxton Pointer				B41F	1994					
513	L513CPJ	Volvo B6-50		Plaxton Pointer				B41F	1994					
514	L514CPJ	Volvo B6-50		Plaxton Pointer				B41F	1994					
515	L515CPJ	Volvo B6-50		Plaxton Pointer				B41F	1994					
516	L516CPJ	Volvo B6-50		Plaxton Pointer				B41F	1994					

610-622		Volvo B10M-50		East Lancs				H49/39F	1989					
610	G610BPH	**612**	G612BPH	**614**	G614BPH	**616**	G616BPH	**618**	G618BPH	**620**	G620BPH	**622**	G622BPH	
611	G611BPH	**613**	G613BPH	**615**	G615BPH	**617**	G617BPH	**619**	G619BPH	**621**	G621BPH			

701	M701HPF	Volvo Olympian YN2RC16Z4		East Lancs				H44/30F	1994					
702	M702HPF	Volvo Olympian YN2RC16Z4		East Lancs				H44/30F	1994					
703	M703HPF	Volvo Olympian YN2RC16Z4		East Lancs				H44/30F	1994					
704	M704HPF	Volvo Olympian YN2RC16Z4		East Lancs				H44/30F	1994					
901	F571SMG	Leyland Olympian ONLXB/1RZ		Alexander RL				H47/32F	1988	Ex Alder Valley South, 1990				
907	F577SMG	Leyland Olympian ONLXB/1RZ		Alexander RL				H47/32F	1988	Ex Alder Valley South, 1990				

908	F578SMG	Leyland Olympian ONLXB/1RZ	Alexander RL		H47/32F	1988	Ex Alder Valley South, 1990
910	F580SMG	Leyland Olympian ONLXB/1RZ	Alexander RL		H47/32F	1988	Ex Alder Valley South, 1990
3713	TOF713S	Leyland National 11351A/1R			B49F	1978	Ex Tellings-Golden Miller, Byfleet, 1992
4556	A156EPA	Leyland Tiger TRCTL11/3R	Plaxton Paramount 3200 Exp		C57F	1984	Ex Southend, 1997
4713t	LPB218P	Leyland National 10351/1R			B41F	1976	Ex Southend, 1997
4716t	GGE156T	Leyland National 10351A/1R			B41F	1979	Ex Southend, 1997
4721	GGE165T	Leyland National 10351A/1R			B41F	1979	Ex Southend, 1993
25107	H107JAR	Volvo B10M-60	Ikarus		C49FT	1990	Ex Colchester, 1993

Previous registrations

ESK987	B812JPN	**OYD693**	F618HGO	**SIB1278**	BPL481T
ESK988	B815JPN	**PDZ6263**	NOE562R	**SIB6709**	LFR865X
IIL2168	SGR134R	**PDZ6264**	ERP551T	**SIB6711**	HPF310N
JIL2190	JOX499P	**PDZ6265**	GPJ891N	**SIB6713**	UPE215M
JIL2193	RKE520M	**PDZ6273**	JOX490P	**SIB6714**	WPG216M
JIL2196	KDW332P	**PDZ6274**	UHG744R	**SJI5066**	NEN961R
JIL2197	BCD808L	**PDZ6275**	UFG54S	**SJI5569**	NPJ471R
JIL2198	SCK703P	**PDZ6276**	GOL403N	**SJI5570**	JOX491P
JIL2199	UHG736R	**PDZ6277**	TPE161S	**SJI5571**	SCK709P
JIL5367	NOE598R	**RDZ4278**	JOX481P	**SJI5572**	LPF601P
LIL2180	KPA375P	**RDZ4279**	KPA380P		

Special liveries

Allover advertisements: AN184, AN201/29, DD2, DSL37, LR14, LR504, SNB427, 258
Blue Saloon: BS407
Countryliner: BS820, DFC1-4, SR89/90, TC426, TDL46, 168, 25107
Green Line: BTL44, TP91, TPL54
Guildford Link: DSL97-100/5, 236, 402-5
Kent Karrier: MM468/70/1
Route X38 livery: 466/7
Southend: 4556/713/6
Traditional liveries: GS13, RMA16, RMC4, RP21, RT3775

ARRIVA THE SHIRES

1005u	F273CEY	Iveco Daily 49.10	Robin Hood City Nippy	B21F	1988	Ex Crosville Wales, 1995
1006s	F689RKX	Iveco Daily 49.10	Carlyle	B25F	1988	Ex Crosville Wales, 1995
1007s	F266CEY	Iveco Daily 49.10	Robin Hood City Nippy	B21F	1988	Ex Crosville Wales, 1995
1008s	F696CMA	Iveco Daily 49.10	Robin Hood City Nippy	B21F	1988	Ex Crosville Wales, 1995
1108	J976AKY	Ford Transit	Advanced Vehicle Builders	8	1992	Ex Checker, Garston, 1997
1203t	RDS83W	Volvo B58-56	Duple Dominant	B53F	1980	Ex Buffalo, Flitwick, 1995
1204t	RDS84W	Volvo B58-56	Duple Dominant	B53F	1980	Ex Buffalo, Flitwick, 1995
1205t	NJF204W	Bedford YMQ	Plaxton	C45F	1980	Ex Lee & District, 1990
1207s	F657KNL	Iveco Daily 49.10	Carlyle	B23F	1989	Ex OK, Bishop Auckland, 1994

2001-2009		MCW Metrorider MF150/81	MCW		B23F	1988	Ex London Country North West, 1990

2001w	E971DNK	2002	E972DNK	2003	E973DNK	2005	E975DNK	2006	E976DNK	2007	E977DNK	2009	E979DNK

2012	LIL2288	Mercedes-Benz L307D	Reeve Burgess	B12F	1984	Ex Lucketts, Watford, 1997
2013w	D203RGH	Volkswagen LT55	Optare CityPacer	B25F	1987	Ex Lucketts, Watford, 1997
2014w	D989JYG	Volkswagen LT55	Optare CityPacer	DP20FL	1986	Ex Lucketts, Watford, 1997
2015	E985DNK	MCW Metrorider MF150/81	Metro-Cammell-Weymann	B23F	1988	Ex London Country North West, 1990
2016	E986DNK	MCW Metrorider MF150/81	Metro-Cammell-Weymann	B23F	1988	Ex London Country North West, 1990
2018w	E988DNK	MCW Metrorider MF150/81	Metro-Cammell-Weymann	B23F	1988	Ex London Country North West, 1990

2020-2027		MCW Metrorider MF150/83	Metro-Cammell-Weymann		B23F	1988	Ex London Country North West, 1990

2020	E990DNK	2021	E991DNK	2022	E992DNK	2023	E993DNK	2024	E994DNK	2025	E995DNK	2027	E997DNK

2031	D23RPP	Iveco Daily 49.10	Robin Hood	B21F	1987	Ex London Country North West, 1990
2033	E486CNM	MCW Metrorider MF150/74	Metro-Cammell-Weymann	B23F	1988	Ex Sovereign, 1990
2037	F122TRU	Mercedes-Benz 709D	Reeve Burgess	B25F	1988	Ex Kentish Bus, 1991
2038	F123TRU	Mercedes-Benz 709D	Reeve Burgess	B25F	1988	Ex Metrobus, Orpington,1991
2039	F124TRU	Mercedes-Benz 709D	Reeve Burgess	B25F	1988	Ex Kentish Bus, 1991
2040	F125TRU	Mercedes-Benz 709D	Reeve Burgess	B25F	1988	Ex Metrobus, Orpington, 1991
2041	E341DRO	Iveco Daily 49.10	Dormobile	B25F	1988	
2043	F128TRU	Mercedes-Benz 709D	Reeve Burgess	B25F	1988	Ex Metrobus, Orpington, 1991
2045	E335DRO	Iveco Daily 49.10	Dormobile	B25F	1988	
2048	F598CET	Mercedes-Benz 609D	Reeve Burgess	C25F	1988	Ex Clydeside 2000, 1992
2049	F287FLG	Iveco Daily 49.10	Carlyle	B23F	1988	Ex Buffalo, Flitwick, 1995
2050	G58BEL	Mercedes-Benz 811D	Wadham Stringer	DP31F	1989	Ex Buffalo, Flitwick, 1995
2051	F985GKJ	Iveco Daily 49.10	Robin Hood	B25F	1989	Ex Buffalo, Flitwick, 1995
2052	MBZ6455	Iveco Daily 49.10	Carlyle	B25F	1988	Ex Buffalo, Flitwick, 1995
2053	F969GKJ	Iveco Daily 49.10	Robin Hood	B21F	1989	Ex Buffalo, Flitwick, 1995
2054	G360FOP	Mercedes-Benz 709D	Carlyle	B25F	1989	Ex Mott, Stoke Mandeville, 1995
2055	G896TGG	Mercedes-Benz 811D	Reeve Burgess	B33F	1989	Ex Stevensons, Uttoxeter, 1995
2056	H523SWE	Mercedes-Benz 709D	Whittaker	B29F	1990	Ex Rhondda, 1995

2057	H407FGS	Mercedes-Benz 811D	Reeve Burgess	B31F	1991	Ex Sovereign, 1996
2058	H408FGS	Mercedes-Benz 811D	Reeve Burgess	B31F	1991	Ex Sovereign, 1996
2059	H406FGS	Mercedes-Benz 811D	Reeve Burgess	B31F	1990	Ex Sovereign, 1996
2060	H848AUS	Mercedes-Benz 709D	Dormobile	B29F	1991	Ex Clydeside 2000, 1992
2061	H641UWE	Mercedes-Benz 811D	Whittaker	B31F	1991	Ex Buffalo, Flitwick, 1995
2062	H642UWE	Mercedes-Benz 811D	Whittaker	B31F	1991	Ex Buffalo, Flitwick, 1995
2063	H35DGD	Mercedes-Benz 811D	Dormobile	B33F	1991	Ex Pathfinder, Newark, 1995
2064	H614CGG	Mercedes-Benz 709D	Dormobile	B33F	1991	Ex Pathfinder, Newark, 1995
2065	F121TRU	Mercedes-Benz 709D	Reeve Burgess	B25F	1988	Ex Kentish Bus, 1991
2066	J917HGD	Mercedes-Benz 709D	Dormobile	B29F	1991	Ex Clydeside 2000, 1992
2067	H231KBH	Mercedes-Benz 709D	Carlyle	B27F	1991	Ex Buffalo, Flitwick, 1995
2068	H408BVR	Mercedes-Benz 709D	Reeve Burgess	B25F	1990	Ex Arrowline, Knutsford, 1995
2069	H409BVR	Mercedes-Benz 709D	Reeve Burgess	B25F	1990	Ex Arrowline, Knutsford, 1995
2070	J65UNA	Mercedes-Benz 709D	Reeve Burgess	B25F	1992	Ex South Lancashire, St Helens, 1996
2071	K8BUS	Mercedes-Benz 811D	Wright	B33F	1992	Ex Patterson, Birmingham, 1995
2072	K578YOJ	Mercedes-Benz 709D	Dormobile	B29F	1993	Ex Patterson, Birmingham, 1995
2073	K543OGA	Mercedes-Benz 709D	Dormobile	B29F	1992	Ex Midland Fox, 1995
2074	K579YOJ	Mercedes-Benz 709D	Dormobile	B29F	1993	Ex Patterson, Birmingham, 1995
2075	K25WND	Mercedes-Benz 609D	Made-to-Measure	B24F	1992	Ex Birmingham Omnibus, Tividale, 1995
2076	K26WND	Mercedes-Benz 609D	Made-to-Measure	B24F	1992	Ex Birmingham Omnibus, Tividale, 1995
2077	K27WND	Mercedes-Benz 609D	Made-to-Measure	B24F	1992	Ex Birmingham Omnibus, Tividale, 1995
2078	K28WND	Mercedes-Benz 609D	Made-to-Measure	B24F	1992	Ex Birmingham Omnibus, Tividale, 1995
2079	K29WND	Mercedes-Benz 609D	Made-to-Measure	B24F	1992	Ex Birmingham Omnibus, Tividale, 1995
2080	K580YOJ	Mercedes-Benz 811D	Wright	B33F	1992	Ex Patterson, Birmingham, 1995
2081	K31WND	Mercedes-Benz 609D	Made-to-Measure	B24F	1992	Ex Birmingham Omnibus, Tividale, 1995
2082	K32WND	Mercedes-Benz 609D	Made-to-Measure	B24F	1992	Ex Birmingham Omnibus, Tividale, 1995
2083	K203FEH	Mercedes-Benz 709D	Dormobile	B27F	1993	Ex Stevensons, Uttoxeter, 1995
2084	L864BEA	Iveco Daily 49.10	Marshall C29	B23F	1993	Ex Buffalo, Flitwick, 1995
2085	L863BEA	Iveco Daily 49.10	Marshall C29	B23F	1993	Ex Buffalo, Flitwick, 1995
2086	L326AUT	Mercedes-Benz 709D	Leicester Carriage Builders	B25F	1994	Ex Midland Fox, 1994
2087	L327AUT	Mercedes-Benz 709D	Leicester Carriage Builders	B25F	1994	Ex Midland Fox, 1994
2088	L328AUT	Mercedes-Benz 709D	Leicester Carriage Builders	B25F	1994	Ex Midland Fox, 1994
2089	K202FEH	Mercedes-Benz 709D	Dormobile	B27F	1993	Ex Stevensons, Uttoxeter, 1995
2090	M150RBH	Iveco Daily 59.12	Marshall	B27F	1994	
2091	M151RBH	Iveco Daily 59.12	Marshall	B27F	1994	
2092	M152RBH	Iveco Daily 59.12	Marshall	B27F	1994	
2093	M153RBH	Iveco Daily 59.12	Marshall	B27F	1994	
2094	M154RBH	Iveco Daily 59.12	Marshall	B27F	1994	
2095	K184GDU	Mercedes-Benz 811D	Wright	B31F	1993	Ex Mott, Stoke Mandeville, 1995
2096	M156RBH	Iveco Daily 59.12	Marshall C31	B27F	1994	
2097	M157RBH	Iveco Daily 59.12	Marshall C31	B27F	1994	
2098	M158RBH	Iveco Daily 59.12	Marshall C31	B27F	1994	
2099	M159RBH	Iveco Daily 59.12	Marshall C31	B27F	1994	
2100	M160RBH	Iveco Daily 59.12	Marshall C31	B27F	1994	

2101	J171GGG	Mercedes-Benz 709D	Dormobile	B29F	1991	Ex Mott, Stoke Mandeville, 1995
2102	L600BUS	Optare MetroRider MR11	Optare	B31F	1995	Ex Lucketts, Watford, 1997
2103	L700BUS	Optare MetroRider MR11	Optare	B32F	1996	Ex Lucketts, Watford, 1997
2104	L800BUS	Optare MetroRider MR11	Optare	B31F	1996	Ex Lucketts, Watford, 1997
2105	M45WUR	Mercedes-Benz 709D	Plaxton	B27F	1995	
2106	M46WUR	Mercedes-Benz 709D	Plaxton	B27F	1995	
2107	M47WUR	Mercedes-Benz 709D	Plaxton	B27F	1995	
2108	M38WUR	Mercedes-Benz 709D	Plaxton	DP31F	1995	
2109	M39WUR	Mercedes-Benz 709D	Plaxton	DP31F	1995	
2110	N920ETM	Mercedes-Benz 709D	Plaxton	B27F	1995	
2111	M41WUR	Mercedes-Benz 709D	Plaxton	DP31F	1995	
2112	M42WUR	Mercedes-Benz 709D	Plaxton	DP31F	1995	

2113-2162		Mercedes-Benz 709D	Plaxton	B27F*	1995/6	* 2115/6 are DP27F

2113	M43WUR	2121	N191EMJ	2129	N909ETM	2137	N917ETM	2145	N375JGS	2153	N383JGS	2161	P671PNM
2114	N918ETM	2122	N192EMJ	2130	N910ETM	2138	N368JGS	2146	N376JGS	2154	N384JGS	2162	P669PNM
2115	N919ETM	2123	N193EMJ	2131	N911ETM	2139	N369JGS	2147	N377JGS	2155	N385JGS		
2116	N186EMJ	2124	N194EMJ	2132	N912ETM	2140	N370JGS	2148	N378JGS	2156	N386JGS		
2117	N187EMJ	2125	N195EMJ	2133	N913ETM	2141	N371JGS	2149	N379JGS	2157	N387JGS		
2118	N188EMJ	2126	N196EMJ	2134	N914ETM	2142	N372JGS	2150	N380JGS	2158	N366JGS		
2119	N189EMJ	2127	N907ETM	2135	N915ETM	2143	N373JGS	2151	N381JGS	2159	N367JGS		
2120	N190EMJ	2128	N908ETM	2136	N916ETM	2144	N374JGS	2152	N382JGS	2160	P670PNM		

2163t	D208SKD	Mercedes-Benz L608D	Reeve Burgess	B18F	1986	Ex London & Country, 1997
2164t	D210SKD	Mercedes-Benz L608D	Reeve Burgess	B18F	1986	Ex London & Country, 1997
2165	WIB1114	Mercedes-Benz 609D	PMT	C26F	1987	Ex Checker, Garston, 1997
2166	J465UFJ	Mercedes-Benz 609D	Crystals	C24F	1992	Ex Checker, Garston, 1997
2167	SLU261	Ford Transit	Williams Deansgate	12	1987	Ex Checker, Garston, 1997
2168	G40OHS	Ford Transit	Dormobile	B16F	1989	Ex Checker, Garston, 1997
2169	G735PGA	Ford Transit	Williams Deansgate	B14F	1989	Ex Checker, Garston, 1997
2170	J964NLL	Ford Transit	Crystals	B13F	1992	Ex Checker, Garston, 1997

2171-2184		Mercedes-Benz O814D	Plaxton Beaver 2	B27F	1997	

2171	R171VBM	2173	R173VBM	2175	R175VBM	2177	R177VBM	2179	R179VBM	2181	R181VBM	2183	R183VBM
2172	R172VBM	2174	R174VBM	2176	R176VBM	2178	R178VBM	2180	R180VBM	2182	R182VBM	2184	R184VBM

2801	LAZ5765	Mercedes-Benz L608D	Reeve Burgess	B20F	1986	Ex Clydeside, 1997
2802	LAZ5785	Mercedes-Benz L608D	Alexander AM	B20F	1986	Ex Clydeside, 1997
2803	LAZ5929	Mercedes-Benz L608D	Rootes	B20F	1986	Ex Clydeside, 1997
2804	LAZ5962	Mercedes-Benz L608D	Rootes	B20F	1986	Ex Clydeside, 1997
2805	LAZ5964	Mercedes-Benz L608D	Reeve Burgess	B20F	1986	Ex Clydeside, 1997
2806	LAZ6771	Mercedes-Benz L608D	Rootes	B20F	1986	Ex Clydeside, 1997
2807	C206EKJ	Mercedes-Benz L608D	Rootes	B20F	1986	Ex Clydeside, 1997
2808	HIL8438	Mercedes-Benz L608D	Rootes	B20F	1986	Ex Clydeside, 1997

2809	HIL8439	Mercedes-Benz L608D	Rootes				B20F	1986	Ex Clydeside, 1997
2810	D36KKP	Mercedes-Benz L608D	Rootes				B20F	1986	Ex Clydeside, 1997
2811	D203SKD	Mercedes-Benz L608D	Reeve Burgess				DP19F	1986	Ex Clydeside, 1997
2812	D206SKD	Mercedes-Benz L608D	Reeve Burgess				DP19F	1986	Ex Clydeside, 1997
2813	D440UHC	Mercedes-Benz L608D	Alexander AM				B20F	1986	Ex Crosville Wales, 1997
2814	D960UDY	Mercedes-Benz L608D	Reeve Burgess				B20F	1986	Ex Crosville Wales, 1997
3010	KNV513P	Leyland National 11351/1R					B49F	1976	Ex United Counties, 1986
3014	SBD524R	Leyland National 11351A/1R					B49F	1977	Ex United Counties, 1986
3015	BVV545T	Leyland National 11351A/1R					DP49F	1978	Ex United Counties, 1986
3016w	BVV542T	Leyland National 11351A/1R					B49F	1978	Ex United Counties, 1986
3017w	XVV537S	Leyland National 11351A/1R					B49F	1978	Ex United Counties, 1986
3018w	XVV538S	Leyland National 11351A/1R					B49F	1978	Ex United Counties, 1986
3026w	MNH569V	Leyland National 11351A/1R					B49F	1979	Ex United Counties, 1986
3027	MNH577V	Leyland National 11351A/1R					B49F	1979	Ex United Counties, 1986
3031	NRP581V	Leyland National 2 NL116L11/1R					B49F	1980	Ex United Counties, 1986
3033	SVV588W	Leyland National 2 NL116L11/1R					B49F	1980	Ex United Counties, 1986
3035-3043		Leyland National 2 NL106AL11/2R					B44F	1981	Ex Parfitt, Rhymney, 1995
3035	GUW465W	**3037**	GUW457W	**3039**	GUW447W	**3041**	GUW461W	**3043**	GUW475W
3036	GUW456W	**3038**	GUW441W	**3040**	GUW494W	**3042**	GUW462W		
3044	IIL4821	Leyland National 10351/1R/SC	East Lancs (1993)				B41F	1974	Ex Crosville Wales, 1995
3045	IIL4822	Leyland National 10351/1R/SC	East Lancs (1993)				B41F	1976	Ex Crosville Wales, 1995
3046	TIB4873	Leyland National 10351B/1R	East Lancs (1993)				B41F	1979	Ex Crosville Wales, 1995
3047	IIL4824	Leyland National 10351/1R	East Lancs (1993)				B41F	1975	Ex Crosville Wales, 1995
3048	BAZ6869	Leyland National 10351B/1R	East Lancs (1994)				B41F	1979	Ex Crosville Wales, 1995
3049	RJI6861	Leyland National 10351B/1R	East Lancs (1994)				B41F	1979	Ex Crosville Wales, 1995
3050	BTX152T	Leyland National 10351A/2R	East Lancs (1994)				B44F	1979	Ex Parfitt, Rhymney, 1995
3051	IAZ3457	Leyland National 11351A/1R					B47FL	1978	Ex United Counties, 1986
3052	IAZ4037	Leyland National 11351A/1R					B49F	1977	Ex United Counties, 1986; DAF engine, Volvo badge
3053	CAZ6852	Leyland National 10351B/1R	East Lancs (1994)				B41F	1978	Ex Crosville Wales, 1995
3054	TIB7835	Leyland National 10351B/1R	East Lancs (1994)				B41F	1979	Ex Crosville Wales, 1995
3055	RJI6862	Leyland National 10351B/1R	East Lancs (1994)				B41F	1979	Ex Crosville Wales, 1995
3056	IIL4823	Leyland National 10351/1R	East Lancs (1993)				B41F	1978	Ex Crosville Wales, 1995
3057	TIB4886	Leyland National 10351/1R/SC	East Lancs (1993)				B41F	1975	Ex Crosville Wales, 1995
3058	GHB574V	Volvo B58-61	East Lancs				B53F	1980	Ex Parfitt, Rhymney, 1995
3059u	HIL7467	Volvo B10M-61	East Lancs (1991)				B55F	1983	Ex Buffalo, Flitwick, 1995
3060u	MBZ6454	Volvo B10M-61	East Lancs (1991)				B55F	1985	Ex Buffalo, Flitwick, 1995
3061	D603ACW	Leyland Lynx LX112L10ZR1	Leyland				B51F	1987	Ex Sovereign, 1990
3062	E970NMK	Leyland Lynx LX112TL11ZR1	Leyland				B49F	1987	Ex Sovereign, 1990
3063	E420EBH	Leyland Lynx LX112TL11ZR1R	Leyland				B51F	1988	Ex Sovereign, 1996
3064	E969PME	Leyland Lynx LX112L10ZR1	Leyland				B49F	1988	Ex Atlas, London NW10, 1994

3065	E965PME	Leyland Lynx LX112TL11ZR1	Leyland			B49F	1988	Ex Mott, Stoke Mandeville, 1995			
3066	E966PME	Leyland Lynx LX112TL11ZR1	Leyland			B49F	1988	Ex Mott, Stoke Mandeville, 1995			
3067	H407ERO	Leyland Lynx LX2R11C15Z4R	Leyland			DP45F	1990				
3068	H408ERO	Leyland Lynx LX2R11C15Z4R	Leyland			DP45F	1990				
3069	H409ERO	Leyland Lynx LX2R11C15Z4R	Leyland			DP45F	1990				
3070	H410ERO	Leyland Lynx LX2R11C15Z4R	Leyland			DP45F	1990				
3071	F401PUR	Leyland Lynx LX112L10ZR1R	Leyland			B51F	1989				
3072	F402PUR	Leyland Lynx LX112L10ZR1R	Leyland			B51F	1989				
3073	F403PUR	Leyland Lynx LX112L10ZR1R	Leyland			B51F	1989				
3074	F404PUR	Leyland Lynx LX112L10ZR1R	Leyland			B51F	1989				
3075	F400PUR	Leyland Lynx LX112L10ZR1R	Leyland			B51F	1989				
3076	E970PME	Leyland Lynx LX112L10ZR1	Leyland			B49F	1988	Ex Atlas, London NW10, 1994			
3077	NIB8459	Volvo B10M-61	East Lancs (1991)			B55F	1988	Ex Buffalo, Flitwick, 1995			
3078	F314RMH	Volvo B10M-56	Plaxton			B54F	1988	Ex Buffalo, Flitwick, 1995			
3079	F151KGS	Volvo B10M-56	Plaxton			B54F	1988	Ex Buffalo, Flitwick, 1995			
3080	F152KGS	Volvo B10M-56	Plaxton			B54F	1988	Ex Buffalo, Flitwick, 1995			
3081	F153KGS	Volvo B10M-56	Plaxton			B54F	1988	Ex Buffalo, Flitwick, 1995			
3087t	G97VMM	Leyland Swift LBM6T/2RS	Wadham Stringer			B39F	1989	Ex London Country North West, 1990			
3089	L133HVS	Volvo B10B-58	Alexander AF			B50F	1993	Ex Buffalo, Flitwick, 1995			
3090	M247SPP	Dennis Dart 9.8SDL3054	Wright Handybus			B40F	1994				

3091-3098		Dennis Dart 9.8SDL3004	Carlyle		B40F*	1991	* 3098 is DP39F	

3091	H922LOX	3093	H925LOX	3095	H242MUK	3097	H244MUK	3098	H245MUK
3092	H923LOX	3094	H926LOX	3096	H243MUK				

3099	K447XPA	Dennis Dart 9.8SDL3017	Plaxton Pointer	B40F	1992	Ex Buffalo, Flitwick, 1995
3100	K448XPA	Dennis Dart 9.8SDL3017	Plaxton Pointer	B40F	1992	Ex Buffalo, Flitwick, 1995
3101	L100BUS	Dennis Dart 9.8SDL3035	Plaxton Pointer	B39F	1994	Ex Lucketts, Watford, 1997
3102	L200BUS	Dennis Dart 9.8SDL3035	Plaxton Pointer	B39F	1994	Ex Lucketts, Watford, 1997
3103	L300BUS	Dennis Dart 9SDL3031	Marshall C36	B34F	1994	Ex Lucketts, Watford, 1997
3104	L400BUS	Dennis Dart 9SDL3031	Marshall C36	B34F	1994	Ex Lucketts, Watford, 1997

3105-3136		Volvo B6-50	Northern Counties Paladin	B40F	1994	

3105	L305HPP	3110	L310HPP	3115	L315HPP	3120	M720OMJ	3125	M725OMJ	3130	M710OMJ	3135	M715OMJ
3106	L306HPP	3111	L311HPP	3116	L316HPP	3121	M721OMJ	3126	M726OMJ	3131	M711OMJ	3136	M716OMJ
3107	L307HPP	3112	L312HPP	3117	M717OMJ	3122	M722OMJ	3127	M727OMJ	3132	M712OMJ		
3108	L308HPP	3113	L313HPP	3118	M718OMJ	3123	M723OMJ	3128	M728OMJ	3133	M713OMJ		
3109	L309HPP	3114	L314HPP	3119	M719OMJ	3124	M724OMJ	3129	M729OMJ	3134	M714OMJ		

3137	L43MEH		Volvo B6-50			Plaxton Pointer			B40F		1994	Ex Stevensons, Uttoxeter, 1994
3138	L922LJO		Volvo B6-50			Northern Counties Paladin			B40F		1994	Ex Mott, Stoke Mandeville, 1995
3139	L923LJO		Volvo B6-50			Northern Counties Paladin			B40F		1994	Ex Mott, Stoke Mandeville, 1995
3140	M248SPP		Dennis Dart 9.8SDL3054			Wright Handybus			B40F		1994	
3141	M251SPP		Dennis Dart 9.8SDL3054			Wright Handybus			B40F		1994	
3142	M249SPP		Dennis Dart 9.8SDL3054			Wright Handybus			B40F		1994	

3143-3149			Scania L113CRL			East Lancs Cityzen			B51F		1995	
3143	N693EUR	3144	N694EUR	3145	N695EUR	3146	N696EUR	3147	N697EUR	3148	N698EUR	3149	N699EUR

3150	M250SPP		Dennis Dart 9.8SDL3054			Wright Handybus			B40F		1994	

3151-3170			Scania L113CRL			East Lancs Cityzen			DP49F*		1995	* 3163-3170 are B51F
3151	N701EUR	3154	N704EUR	3157	N707EUR	3160	N710EUR	3163	N713EUR	3166	N716EUR	3169	N31KGS
3152	N702EUR	3155	N705EUR	3158	N708EUR	3161	N711EUR	3164	N714EUR	3167	N28KGS	3170	N32KGS
3153	N703EUR	3156	N706EUR	3159	N709EUR	3162	N712EUR	3165	N715EUR	3168	N29KGS		

3171	P671OPP		Dennis Dart SFD322BR1			East Lancs Spryte			B41F		1996	
3172	P672OPP		Dennis Dart SFD322BR1			East Lancs Spryte			B41F		1996	
3173	P673OPP		Dennis Dart SFD322BR1			East Lancs Spryte			B41F		1996	
3174	P674OPP		Dennis Dart SFD322BR1			East Lancs Spryte			B41F		1996	

3175-3190			Dennis Dart SFD322BR1			Plaxton Pointer			B39F*		1997	* 3175-3178 are B41F
3175	P175SRO	3178	P178SRO	3181	P181SRO	3184	P184SRO	3187	P187SRO	3190	P190SRO		
3176	P176SRO	3179	P179SRO	3182	P182SRO	3185	P185SRO	3188	P188SRO				
3177	P177SRO	3180	P180SRO	3183	P183SRO	3186	P186SRO	3189	P189SRO				

3191-3205			Scania L113CRL			Northern Counties Paladin			DP47F*		1997	* 3191-3195 are B51F
3191	R191RBM	3193	R193RBM	3195	R195RBM	3197	R197RBM	3199	R199RBM	3202	R202RBM	3204	R204RBM
3192	R192RBM	3194	R194RBM	3196	R196RBM	3198	R198RBM	3201	R201RBM	3203	R203RBM	3205	R205RBM

3206-3215			Dennis Dart SFD212BR1			Plaxton Pointer			B31F		1997	
3206	R206GMJ	3208	R208GMJ	3210	R210GMJ	3212	R212GMJ	3214	R214GMJ				
3207	R207GMJ	3209	R209GMJ	3211	R211GMJ	3213	R213GMJ	3215	R215GMJ				

4002	A152EPA		Leyland Tiger TRCTL11/3R		Plaxton Paramount 3200 Exp		C57F	1984	Ex London Country North West, 1990
4003	A153EPA		Leyland Tiger TRCTL11/3R		Plaxton Paramount 3200 Exp		C53F	1984	Ex London Country North West, 1990
4004u	HIL2358		Bedford YNT		Plaxton		C49FT	1982	Ex Lucketts, Watford, 1997
4005	A155EPA		Leyland Tiger TRCTL11/3R		Plaxton Paramount 3200 Exp		C53F	1984	Ex London Country North West, 1990
4006	A113EPA		Leyland Tiger TRCTL11/2RH		Plaxton Paramount 3200 Exp		C53F	1983	Ex London Country North West, 1990
4007	A157EPA		Leyland Tiger TRCTL11/3R		Plaxton Paramount 3200 Exp		C57F	1984	Ex London Country North West, 1990
4008	A143EPA		Leyland Tiger TRCTL11/3R		Plaxton Paramount 3200 Exp		C51F	1984	Ex London Country North West, 1990
4009	FIL4919		Volvo B10M-61		Duple		C49FT	1987	Ex Lucketts, Watford, 1997

4010	A150EPA		Leyland Tiger TRCTL11/3R		Plaxton Paramount 3200 Exp			C51F	1984	Ex London Country North West, 1990	
4011u	DIL7916		Bedford YNV		Duple			C57F	1987	Ex Lucketts, Watford, 1997	
4012	B292KPF		Leyland Tiger TRCTL11/3RH		Plaxton Paramount 3200 2			C51F	1985	Ex London Country North West, 1990	
4013	B293KPF		Leyland Tiger TRCTL11/3RH		Plaxton Paramount 3200 2			C51F	1985	Ex London Country North West, 1990	
4015	HIL7595		Volvo B10M-61		Plaxton			C53F	1988	Ex Moor-Dale, Newcastle, 1994	
4016	SIB4846		Leyland Tiger TRCTL11/3ARZA		Plaxton			C53F	1988	Ex London Country North West, 1990	
4017	C147SPE		Leyland Tiger TRCTL11/3RH		Berkhof Everest 370			C53F	1986	Ex London Country North West, 1990	
4018	C148SPE		Leyland Tiger TRCTL11/3RH		Berkhof Everest 370			C53F	1986	Ex London Country North West, 1990	
4019	C149SPE		Leyland Tiger TRCTL11/3RH		Berkhof Everest 370			C53F	1986	Ex London Country North West, 1990	
4020	SIB7480		Leyland Tiger TRCL10/3ARZA		Plaxton			C51FT	1988	Ex London Country North West, 1990	
4021	E881YKY		Leyland Tiger TRCTL11/3ARZ		Plaxton			C53F	1988		
4022	E882YKY		Leyland Tiger TRCTL11/3ARZ		Plaxton			C53F	1988		
4023	E323OMG		Leyland Tiger TRCTL11/3ARZA		Plaxton Paramount 3200 3			C53F	1988	Ex London Country North West, 1990	
4025	SIB8529		Leyland Tiger TRCL10/3ARZA		Plaxton			C51FT	1988	Ex London Country North West, 1990	
4026	SIB7481		Leyland Tiger TRCL10/3ARZA		Plaxton			C51FT	1988	Ex London Country North West, 1990	
4027	HIL7597		Volvo B10M-61		Plaxton			C53F	1988	Ex Moor-Dale, Newcastle, 1994	
4028	MIL2350		Dennis Javelin 12SDA1919		Duple			C57F	1990	Ex Lucketts, Watford, 1997	
4034	H198AOD		Volvo B10M-60		Plaxton Expressliner			C50FT	1991	Ex Trathens, Plymouth, 1996	
4035	H199AOD		Volvo B10M-60		Plaxton Expressliner			C50FT	1991	Ex Trathens, Plymouth, 1996	
4036	L500BUS		Iveco Daily 480.10.21		Wadham Stringer			B47F	1995	Ex Lucketts, Watford, 1997	
4037	P100LOW		Dennis Javelin SFD712BR3		UVG			C55FTL	1996	Ex Lucketts, Watford, 1997	
4038t	ADZ4731		Volvo B10M-56		Plaxton Viewmaster IV			C51F	1982	Ex Checker, Watford, 1997	
4039	WIB1113		Volvo B10M-61		Plaxton Paramount 2			C53F	1985	Ex Checker, Watford, 1997	
4040	YIB2396		Volvo B10M-61		Plaxton Paramount 2			C53F	1986	Ex Checker, Watford, 1997	
4042	WIB1118		Leyland Tiger TRCTL11/3R		Duple			C53F	1983	Ex Checker, Watford, 1997	
4043	YIB2397		Leyland Tiger TRCTL11/3RZ		Duple			C57F	1987	Ex Checker, Watford, 1997	
4044	WIB1115		DAF MB200DKTL600		Plaxton Supreme V			C53F	1983	Ex Checker, Watford, 1997	
4046	TIB 5906		Leyland Tiger TRCTL11/3RH		Duple 320			C51F	1986	Ex Kentish Bus, 1997	

4047-4056			DAF DE33WSSB3000		Plaxton Première 320			C53F	1997		
4047	R447SKX	4049	R449SKX	4051	R451SKX	4053	R453SKX	4055	R455SKX		
4048	R448SKX	4050	R450SKX	4052	R452SKX	4054	R454SKX	4056	R456SKX		

5000	BKE847T		Bristol VRT/SL3/6LXB		Eastern Coach Works			H43/31F	1979	Ex Maidstone & District, 1997	
5011	PRP802M		Bristol VRT/SL2/6LX		Eastern Coach Works			H43/31F	1974	Ex United Counties, 1986	
5013	LDB837P		Bristol VRT/SL3/6LX		Eastern Coach Works			H43/31F	1975	Ex United Counties, 1986	
5014	OVV851R		Bristol VRT/SL3/6LXB		Eastern Coach Works			H43/31F	1976	Ex United Counties, 1986	
5015	TNH865R		Bristol VRT/SL3/6LXB		Eastern Coach Works			H43/31F	1977	Ex United Counties, 1986	
5016	OCY916R		Bristol VRT/SL3/501		Eastern Coach Works			H43/31F	1977	Ex South Wales, 1987	
5017	IAZ3977		Bristol VRT/SL3/501		Eastern Coach Works			H43/31F	1977	Ex South Wales, 1987	

5018-5036 Bristol VRT/SL3/6LXB Eastern Coach Works H43/31F 1976-80 Ex United Counties, 1986

5018	OVV852R	5021	WBD877S	5024	YVV895S	5027w	CBD900T	5030	CBD904T	5034	SNV934W
5019	OVV853R	5022	YVV893S	5025	CBD897T	5028	ONH928V	5032	SNV932W	5035	ONH925V
5020u	OVV855R	5023u	YVV894S	5026	CBD899T	5029	ONH929V	5033	SNV933W	5036	UDM448V

5037	JPE237V	Leyland Atlantean AN68B/1R	Roe	H43/39F	1980	Ex London Country North West, 1990
5038	SNV938W	Bristol VRT/SL3/6LXB	Eastern Coach Works	H43/31F	1980	Ex United Counties, 1986
5039	JPE233V	Leyland Atlantean AN68B/1R	Roe	H43/39F	1980	Ex London Country North West, 1990
5040	JPE236V	Leyland Atlantean AN68B/1R	Roe	H43/39F	1980	Ex London Country North West, 1990
5041	KPJ241W	Leyland Atlantean AN68B/1R	Roe	H43/39F	1980	Ex London Country North West, 1990
5042	KPJ242W	Leyland Atlantean AN68B/1R	Roe	H43/39F	1980	Ex London Country North West, 1990
5043	KPJ243W	Leyland Atlantean AN68B/1R	Roe	H43/39F	1980	Ex London Country North West, 1990
5044u	KPJ244W	Leyland Atlantean AN68B/1R	Roe	H43/39F	1980	Ex London Country North West, 1990
5045	TRN477V	Leyland Atlantean AN68A/1R	Eastern Coach Works	H43/31F	1980	Ex Ribble, 1994
5046	URP946W	Bristol VRT/SL3/6LXB	Eastern Coach Works	H43/31F	1981	Ex United Counties, 1986
5047	URP947W	Bristol VRT/SL3/6LXB	Eastern Coach Works	H43/31F	1981	Ex United Counties, 1986
5049	VVV956W	Bristol VRT/SL3/6LXB	Eastern Coach Works	H43/31F	1981	Ex United Counties, 1986
5050	VVV960W	Bristol VRT/SL3/6LXB	Eastern Coach Works	H43/31F	1981	Ex United Counties, 1986
5051	VVV951W	Bristol VRT/SL3/6LXB	Eastern Coach Works	H43/31F	1981	Ex United Counties, 1986
5052	VVV957W	Bristol VRT/SL3/6LXB	Eastern Coach Works	H43/31F	1981	Ex United Counties, 1986

5053-5064 Leyland Olympian ONLXB/1R Eastern Coach Works H45/32F 1981/2 Ex United Counties, 1986
(5061/3/4 ex Rhondda, 1995)

5053	ARP613X	5055	ARP615X	5057	ARP617X	5059	ARP619X	5061	MUH287X	5063	MUH290X
5054	ARP614X	5056	ARP616X	5058	ARP618X	5060	ARP620X	5062	ARP612X	5064	MUX284X

5065	BPF135Y	Leyland Olympian ONTL11/2R	Roe	H43/29F	1983	Ex Sovereign, 1990
5066	BPF136Y	Leyland Olympian ONTL11/2R	Roe	H43/29F	1983	Ex Sovereign, 1990
5067	IAZ2314	Leyland Olympian ONLXB/1R	Eastern Coach Works	H45/32F	1982	Ex Rhondda, 1995
5068	A141DPE	Leyland Olympian ONTL11/1R	Roe	H43/29F	1983	Ex Sovereign, 1990
5069	A149FPG	Leyland Olympian ONTL11/1R	Roe	H43/29F	1984	Ex London Country North West, 1990
5070	A143DPE	Leyland Olympian ONTL11/2R	Roe	H43/29F	1983	Ex Sovereign, 1990
5071	A151FPG	Leyland Olympian ONTL11/1R	Roe	H43/29F	1984	Ex London Country North West, 1990
5072	A152FPG	Leyland Olympian ONTL11/1R	Roe	H43/29F	1984	Ex London Country North West, 1990
5073	A153FPG	Leyland Olympian ONTL11/1R	Roe	H43/29F	1984	Ex London Country North West, 1990
5074	A154FPG	Leyland Olympian ONTL11/1R	Roe	H43/29F	1984	Ex London Country North West, 1990
5075	A155FPG	Leyland Olympian ONTL11/1R	Roe	H43/29F	1984	Ex London Country North West, 1990
5076	B262LPH	Leyland Olympian ONTL11/2R	Eastern Coach Works	H43/29F	1985	Ex Sovereign, 1990
5077	B273LPH	Leyland Olympian ONTL11/1R	Eastern Coach Works	H43/29F	1985	Ex London Country North West, 1990
5078	A698EAU	Leyland Olympian ONTL11/1R	Northern Counties	H47/33D	1984	Ex Buffalo, Flitwick, 1995
5079	A699EAU	Leyland Olympian ONTL11/1R	Northern Counties	H47/33D	1984	Ex Buffalo, Flitwick, 1995
5080	B270LPH	Leyland Olympian ONTL11/1R	Eastern Coach Works	H43/29F	1985	Ex London Country North West, 1990
5081	B271LPH	Leyland Olympian ONTL11/1R	Eastern Coach Works	H43/29F	1985	Ex London Country North West, 1990

5082	B272LPH	Leyland Olympian ONTL11/1R	Eastern Coach Works					H43/29F	1985	Ex London Country North West, 1990
5083	F633LMJ	Leyland Olympian ONCL10/1RZ	Alexander RL					H47/32F	1988	
5084	F634LMJ	Leyland Olympian ONCL10/1RZ	Alexander RL					H47/32F	1988	
5085	F635LMJ	Leyland Olympian ONCL10/1RZ	Alexander RL					H47/32F	1988	
5086	F636LMJ	Leyland Olympian ONCL10/1RZ	Alexander RL					DPH47/29F	1988	
5087	F637LMJ	Leyland Olympian ONCL10/1RZ	Alexander RL					H47/32F	1988	
5088	F638LMJ	Leyland Olympian ONCL10/1RZ	Alexander RL					H47/32F	1988	
5089	F639LMJ	Leyland Olympian ONCL10/1RZ	Alexander RL					H47/32F	1988	
5090	F640LMJ	Leyland Olympian ONCL10/1RZ	Alexander RL					H47/32F	1988	
5091	F641LMJ	Leyland Olympian ONCL10/1RZ	Alexander RL					DPH47/29F	1988	
5092	F642LMJ	Leyland Olympian ONCL10/1RZ	Alexander RL					H47/32F	1988	
5093	F643LMJ	Leyland Olympian ONCL10/1RZ	Alexander RL					H47/32F	1988	
5094	F644LMJ	Leyland Olympian ONCL10/1RZ	Alexander RL					H47/32F	1988	

5095-5107		Leyland Olympian ON2R50C13Z4	Alexander RL					H47/32F*	1989/90	* 5099-5103 are H47/34F; 5104 is DPH47/29F

5095	G645UPP	5097	G647UPP	5099	G649UPP	5101	G651UPP	5103	G653UPP	5105	G655UPP	5107	G657UPP
5096	G646UPP	5098	G648UPP	5100	G650UPP	5102	G652UPP	5104	G654UPP	5106	G656UPP		

5108	F506OYW	Leyland Olympian ONTL11/1RH	Northern Counties	H47/30F	1988	Ex Mott, Stoke Mandeville, 1995
5109	G129YEV	Leyland Olympian ONCL10/1RZ	Northern Counties	H49/34F	1989	Ex London Country North West, 1990
5110	G130YEV	Leyland Olympian ONCL10/1RZ	Northern Counties	H49/34F	1989	Ex London Country North West, 1990

5111-5125		Leyland Olympian ONCL10/1RZ	Leyland	H47/31F	1989/90	Ex London Country North West, 1990

5111	G281UMJ	5114	G284UMJ	5117	G287UMJ	5120	G290UMJ	5123	G293UMJ
5112	G282UMJ	5115	G285UMJ	5118	G288UMJ	5121	G291UMJ	5124	G294UMJ
5113	G283UMJ	5116	G286UMJ	5119	G289UMJ	5122	G292UMJ	5125	G295UMJ

5126	H196GRO	Leyland Olympian ON2R50C13Z4	Leyland	H47/29F	1991	
5127	H197GRO	Leyland Olympian ON2R50C13Z4	Leyland	H47/29F	1991	
5128	H198GRO	Leyland Olympian ON2R50C13Z4	Leyland	H47/29F	1991	
5129	H199GRO	Leyland Olympian ON2R50C13Z4	Leyland	H47/29F	1991	
5130	F747XCS	Leyland Olympian ONCL10/1RZ	Alexander RL	H47/32F	1989	Ex McMenemy, Ardrossan, 1995
5132	H202GRO	Leyland Olympian ON2R50C13Z4	Leyland	H47/29F	1991	
5133	H203GRO	Leyland Olympian ON2R50C13Z4	Leyland	H47/29F	1991	
5134	G131YWC	Leyland Olympian ONCL10/1RZ	Northern Counties	H49/34F	1989	Ex Ensign, Purfleet, 1991
5135	G132YWC	Leyland Olympian ONCL10/1RZ	Northern Counties	H49/34F	1989	Ex London Country North West, 1990

5136-5145		Volvo Olympian YN2RV18Z4	Northern Counties Palatine 1	H47/30F	1996

5136	N36JPP	5138	N38JPP	5140	N46JPP	5142	N42JPP	5144	N35JPP
5137	N37JPP	5139	N39JPP	5141	N41JPP	5143	N43JPP	5145	N45JPP

5146-5160		Volvo Olympian			Northern Counties Palatine 2		H—F	1998	On order

5146	5149	5152	5155	5158
5147	5150	5153	5156	5159
5148	5151	5154	5157	5160

5866	FKM866V	Bristol VRT/SL3/6LXB	Eastern Coach Works	H43/31F	1979	Ex Maidstone & District, 1997
5874	FKM874V	Bristol VRT/SL3/6LXB	Eastern Coach Works	H43/31F	1979	Ex Maidstone & District, 1997
5905u	BKE855T	Bristol VRT/SL3/6LXB	Eastern Coach Works	H43/31F	1979	Ex Maidstone & District, 1997
5910u	UPK128S	Leyland Atlantean AN68A/1R	Park Royal	H43/30F	1978	Ex London & Country, 1997
5913u	FKM865V	Bristol VRT/SL3/6LXB	Eastern Coach Works	H43/31F	1979	Ex Maidstone & District, 1997
5914u	BKE843T	Bristol VRT/SL3/6LXB	Eastern Coach Works	H43/31F	1978	Ex Maidstone & District, 1997
5916u	GHB84W	Bristol VRT/SL3/6LXB	East Lancs	H44/32F	1981	Ex Maidstone & District, 1997
5917u	BRC835T	Bristol VRT/SL3/6LXB	Eastern Coach Works	H43/31F	1979	Ex Maidstone & District, 1997

Previous registrations

ADZ4731	KNP3X	IIL4822	LPB180P	RJI6861	HMA569T
BAZ6869	JTU577T	IIL4823	GMB659T	RJI6862	MCA677T
BTX152T	AYR329T, NIW4810	IIL4824	HNB20N	SIB4846	E321OMG
CAZ6852	HMA561T	J65UNA	J59MHF, J6SLT	SIB7480	E325OMG
DIL7916	D121EFH	J964NLL	J413UUK	SIB7481	E326OMG
FIL4919	D614FSL, D448FSP	LAZ5765	D650CVN	SIB8529	E324OMG
HIL2358	AEG121Y	LAZ5785	C203PCD	SLU261	WET880, D969MDB
HIL5438	C212EKJ	LAZ5929	C203EKJ	TIB4873	MCA671T
HIL5439	C214EKJ	LAZ5962	C211EKJ	TIB4886	HPF322N
HIL7467	FVA387Y, 3408WY, NRV859Y	LAZ5964	D652CVN	TIB5906	C264SPC
HIL7595	E663UNE	LAZ6771	C207EKJ	TIB7835	JTU594T
HIL7597	E660UNE	LIL2288	B259AMG	WIB1113	B504CGP
IAZ2314	MUH288X	L500BUS	M289OUR	WIB1114	E428YDM
IAZ3457	BVV548T	MBZ6454	B572AVW, URY598	WIB1115	FKK615Y
IAZ3977	RHT917S	MBZ6455	E295VOM, 7178KP	WIB1118	YPD145Y
IAZ4037	VRP532S	MIL2350	G171BLH	YIB2396	C510LGH
IIL4821	XPD299N	NIB8459	E637NEL	YIB2397	D296RKW

Special liveries

Airport Link: 3126
Challenger: 2801-14
Checker Travel: 1108, 2165/6/8-70, 4007/38-40/2/4
Dacorum Park & Ride: 2132
Green Line: 4002/3/5/8/10/2/3/5-7/9-23/5/7/46-56
Jetlink: 4018/26/34/5

Lucketts: 2012-4/102/4, 3101-4, 4004/11/28/37
Overall advertisements: 2006/45/70/3/83/6, 2101, 3011/26/44/7/50/3/5/6-8/72/5/95, 3113/20/34/42/52/60/73, 5014/7/30/49/56/63/5/71/3/89, 5100/3/9/38
School Bus: 5011
Training livery: 1203-5/7
White: 2020, 5045

THE BEE LINE

D201-208			Dennis Dart 9.8SDL3017*			Plaxton Pointer			B40F		1993-94 *D206-8 are 9.8SDL3035		
201	K279XJB	**203**	K282XJB	**205**	L205GMO	**207**	L207GMO	**208**	L208GMO				
202	K281XJB	**204**	K283XJB	**206**	L206GMO								

L211-217			Dennis Dart SFD212			Plaxton Pointer			B37F		1996		
211	N211WRD	**212**	N212WRD	**213**	N213WRD	**214**	N214WRD	**215**	N215WRD	**216**	N216WRD	**217**	N217WRD

LA506	G55XLO	Leyland Olympian ONCL10/1RZ	Alexander RL		H47/28F	1989	Ex London Buslines, 1997
LA507	G56XLO	Leyland Olympian ONCL10/1RZ	Alexander RL		H47/28F	1989	Ex London Buslines, 1997

LN501-505			Leyland Olympian ONCL10/1RZ			Northern Counties			H45/29F		1988	
501	F172LBL	**502**	F173LBL	**503**	F174LBL	**504**	F175LBL	**505**	F176LBL			

LS347t	KPA360P	Leyland National 11351/1R		B49F	1975	Ex Thames Valley & Aldershot, 1986
LS362t	TPE162S	Leyland National 11351A/1R		B49F	1978	Ex Thames Valley & Aldershot, 1986
LS364u	TPE165S	Leyland National 11351A/1R		B49F	1978	Ex Thames Valley & Aldershot, 1986
LX800	F101GRM	Leyland Lynx LX112L10ZR1R	Leyland	DP46F	1988	Ex CentreWest, 1996
LX801	K801CAN	Leyland Lynx LX2R11C15Z4S	Leyland	B47F	1992	Ex Alder Valley, 1992
LX802	K802CAN	Leyland Lynx LX2R11C15Z4S	Leyland	B47F	1992	Ex Alder Valley, 1992
LX803	D751DLO	Leyland Lynx LX112TL11ZR1RS	Leyland	B49F	1987	Ex London Buslines, 1995
LX804	D752DLO	Leyland Lynx LX112TL11ZR1RS	Leyland	B49F	1987	Ex London Buslines, 1995
LX805	D753DLO	Leyland Lynx LX112TL11ZR1RS	Leyland	B49F	1987	Ex London Buslines, 1995
LX806	D754DLO	Leyland Lynx LX112TL11ZR1RS	Leyland	B49F	1987	Ex London Buslines, 1995
LX807	809DYE	Leyland Lynx LX112TL11ZR1R	Leyland	DP48F	1987	Ex CentreWest, 1997
LX808	D755DLO	Leyland Lynx LX112TL11ZR1RS	Leyland	B49F	1987	Ex London Buslines, 1995
LX809	292CLT	Leyland Lynx LX112L10ZR1R	Leyland	DP46F	1988	Ex CentreWest, 1997

RW1-53			Renault-Dodge S75			Wright			B28F		1990	Ex CentreWest, 1996/7	
1	HDZ5401	8	HDZ5408	16	HDZ5416	23	HDZ5423	31	HDZ5431	38	HDZ5438	47	HDZ5447
2	HDZ5402	9	HDZ5409	17	HDZ5417	24	HDZ5424	32	HDZ5432	39	HDZ5439	48	HDZ5448
3	HDZ5403	10	HDZ5410	18	HDZ5418	25	HDZ5425	33	HDZ5433	42	HDZ5442	49	HDZ5449
4	HDZ5404	11	HDZ5411	19	HDZ5419	26	HDZ5426	34	HDZ5434	43	HDZ5443	50	HDZ5450
5	HDZ5405	13	HDZ5413	20	HDZ5420	27	HDZ5427	35	HDZ5435	44	HDZ5444	51	HDZ5451
6	HDZ5406	14	HDZ5414	21	HDZ5421	29	HDZ5429	36	HDZ5436	45	HDZ5445	52	HDZ5452
7	HDZ5407	15	HDZ5415	22	HDZ5422	30	HDZ5430	37	HDZ5437	46	HDZ5446	53	HDZ5453

SB740-746			Scania K113CRB			Berkhof Excellence 2000			C53F		1991		
740	TJI4830	**741**	TJI4831	**742**	TJI4832	**743**	TJI4833	**744**	TJI4834	**745**	TJI4835	**746**	TJI4836

SB791-798	Scania K113CRB	Berkhof Excellence 1000	C53F	1995		

791	M791TCF	793	M793TCF	795	N795WAN	797	N797WAN
792	M792TCF	794	M794TCF	796	N796WAN	798	N798WAN

SN810-819	Scania L113CRL*	Northern Counties Paladin	B51F	1995	*810 is L113CLL	

810	M810PGM	812	M812PGM	814	M814PGM	816	M816PGM	818	M818PGM
811	M811PGM	813	M813PGM	815	M815PGM	817	M817PGM	819	M819PGM

VR539	GGM89W	Bristol VRT/SL3/6LXB	Eastern Coach Works	H43/31F	1980	Ex Thames Valley & Aldershot, 1992
VR540	GGM90W	Bristol VRT/SL3/6LXB	Eastern Coach Works	H43/31F	1980	Ex Thames Valley & Aldershot, 1992

TP768	TJI4838	Leyland Tiger TRCTL11/3R	Plaxton Paramount 3200 3	C53F	1988	Ex Luton & District, 1993

VJ782-789	Volvo B10M-60	Jonckheere Jubilee P50	C53F	1989	Ex Alder Valley, 1992	

782	TJI4822	783	TJI4823	786	TJI4826	788	TJI4828	789	TJI4829

VJ790	TJI4820	Volvo B10M-60	Jonckheere Jubilee P50	C53F	1989	

Previous registrations

TJI4820	F760OJH	TJI4830	J740TDP	TJI4835	J745TDP		
TJI4822	F772OJH	TJI4831	J741TDP	TJI4836	J746TDP		
TJI4823	F773OJH	TJI4832	J742TDP	TJI4838	E322OMG		
TJI4826	F756OJH	TJI4833	J743TDP	292CLT	F102GRM		
TJI4828	F758OJH	TJI4834	J744TDP	809DYE	D105NDW		
TJI4829	F759OJH						

Special liveries

Airportlink : D201/2/4-8
Green Line : SB740-6, TP768, VJ782/3/6/8-90
Great Western Trains Railair Link : SB791-8
Legoland Shuttle : L212
Overall advertisements: D203, LA507, LN503/5, LS364, LX807, VR540

20	VDL264K	Bedford YRQ	Plaxton Derwent	B49F	1972	Ex Gale, Haslemere, 1988
24	F70RPL	Mercedes-Benz 811D	Optare StarRider	DP33F	1989	
25	G301CPL	Mercedes-Benz 811D	Optare StarRider	B33F	1989	
26	G972WPA	Optare MetroRider	Optare	B33F	1990	
32	OHV208Y	Ford R1114	Wadham Stringer Vanguard	B33F	1983	Ex London Borough of Lewisham, 1991
33	YLN636S	Ford R1014	Duple Dominant	B47F	1978	Ex London Borough of Hillingdon, 1991
34	J326PPD	Optare MetroRider	Optare	B33F	1991	
36	J752PPM	Dennis Dart 9SDL3002	Wadham Stringer Portsdown	B37F	1991	
37	D602RGJ	Bedford YMT	Plaxton Derwent	B55F	1987	Ex Epsom Buses, 1991
38	D167TAU	Bedford YMT	Duple Dominant	B53F	1987	Ex National Plant, South Normanton, 1992
40	B88BVW	Ford R1015	Wadham Stringer Vanguard	B33F	1985	Ex Wealden PSV, Five Oak Green, 1992
41	C915BYP	Bedford YMP	Wadham Stringer Vanguard	DP45F	1985	Ex Civil Service College, Sunningdale, 1992
45	K488XPG	Dennis Dart 9.8SDL3017	Plaxton Pointer	B40F	1993	
47	L726DPG	Dennis Dart 9.8SDL3035	Plaxton Pointer	B40F	1993	
48	L735MWW	Optare MetroRider	Optare	B29F	1994	
49	L354FPF	Dennis Dart 9.8SDL3035	Plaxton Pointer	B40F	1994	
50	M150HPL	Dennis Dart 9.8SDL3035	Plaxton Pointer	B40F	1994	
51	M151HPL	Dennis Dart 9.8SDL3040	Plaxton Pointer	B40F	1994	
52	M152HPL	Mercedes-Benz 709D	Plaxton Beaver	B25F	1995	
53	M153HPL	Iveco Daily 59.12	WSC	B24FL	1995	
54	E407EPE	Dodge S46	Northern Counties	B22F	1988	Ex London & Country, 1995
55	G105DPB	Renault Dodge S56	Northern Counties	B25F	1989	Ex London & Country, 1996
56	H840GDY	Dennis Dart 9SDL3002	Wadham Stringer Portsdown	B35F	1990	Ex Eastbourne, 1997
57	H908DTP	Dennis Dart 9SDL3002	Wadham Stringer Portsdown	B35F	1991	Ex Eastbourne, 1997
64	F41CWY	Mercedes-Benz 811D	Optare StarRider	B26F	1989	Ex London Central, 1997
65	H841GDY	Dennis Dart 9SDL3002	Wadham Stringer Portsdown	B35F	1990	Ex Eastbourne, 1997
66	F31CWY	Mercedes-Benz 811D	Optare StarRider	B26F	1989	Ex London Central, 1997
u	H161WWT	Optare MetroRider MR03	Optare	B26F	1991	Ex Selkent, 1997
u	H165WWT	Optare MetroRider MR03	Optare	B26F	1991	Ex Selkent, 1997
u	H167WWT	Optare MetroRider MR03	Optare	B26F	1991	Ex Selkent, 1997
u	H168WWT	Optare MetroRider MR03	Optare	B26F	1991	Ex Selkent, 1997
251	J51SNY	Leyland Tiger TRCL10/3ARZM	Plaxton 321	C53F	1991	Ex Bebb, Llantwit Fardre, 1993
320	EYE320V	MCW Metrobus DR101/12	MCW	H43/28D	1980	Ex London General, 1997
321	EYE321V	MCW Metrobus DR101/12	MCW	H43/28D	1980	Ex London General, 1997
957	E957GGX	DAF MB230DKVL615	Duple 320	C57F	1988	

31	BPF131Y	Leyland Olympian ONTL11/1R	Roe					H43/29F	1983	Ex Keighley & District, 1996
32	BPF132Y	Leyland Olympian ONTL11/1R	Roe					H43/29F	1983	Ex London Country North East, 1989
33	BPF133Y	Leyland Olympian ONTL11/1R	Roe					H43/29F	1983	Ex London Country North East, 1989
34	BPF134Y	Leyland Olympian ONTL11/1R	Roe					H43/29F	1983	Ex Keighley & District, 1995
37	BPF137Y	Leyland Olympian ONTL11/1R	Roe					H43/29F	1983	Ex London Country North East, 1989
38	A138DPE	Leyland Olympian ONTL11/1R	Roe					H43/29F	1983	Ex London Country North East, 1989
39	A139DPE	Leyland Olympian ONTL11/1R	Roe					H43/29F	1983	Ex Keighley & District, 1993
40	A140DPE	Leyland Olympian ONTL11/1R	Roe					H43/29F	1983	Ex Keighley & District, 1994
66	B266LPH	Leyland Olympian ONTL11/1R	Eastern Coach Works					H43/29F	1985	Ex Keighley & District, 1997
68	B268LPH	Leyland Olympian ONTL11/1R	Eastern Coach Works					H43/29F	1985	Ex Keighley & District, 1997
69	B269LPH	Leyland Olympian ONTL11/1R	Eastern Coach Works					H43/29F	1985	Ex Keighley & District, 1997

101-105		Volvo B10B-58		Wright Endurance				DP49F	1995	
101	M101UKX	**102**	M102UKX	**103**	M103UKX	**104**	M104UKX	**105**	M105UKX	

106	N106GVS	Volvo B10B-58		Wright Endurance				B51F	1996	
107	N107GVS	Volvo B10B-58		Wright Endurance				B51F	1996	
108	N108GVS	Volvo B10B-58		Wright Endurance				B51F	1996	
109	N109GVS	Volvo B10B-58		Wright Endurance				B51F	1996	
110	M310KHP	Volvo B10B-58		Wright Endurance				B51F	1995	Ex demonstrator, 1996
112	P112RGS	Volvo B10M-58		Wright Endurance				B49F	1997	

201-207		Leyland Lynx LX2R11C15Z4S		Leyland				B49F	1989	
201	G201URO	**202**	G202URO	**203**	G203URO	**204**	G204URO	**205**	G205URO	**206**	G206URO	**207**	G207URO

213	F203MBT	Leyland Lynx LX112TL11ZR1R	Leyland					B49F	1989	Ex Keighley & District, 1993
214	F204MBT	Leyland Lynx LX112TL11ZR1R	Leyland					B49F	1989	Ex Keighley & District, 1993
215	F205MBT	Leyland Lynx LX112TL11ZR1R	Leyland					B47F	1989	Ex Keighley & District, 1992
216	F206MBT	Leyland Lynx LX112TL11ZR1R	Leyland					B49F	1989	Ex Keighley & District, 1993
217	F207MBT	Leyland Lynx LX112TL11ZR1R	Leyland					B49F	1989	Ex Keighley & District, 1993
218	F208MBT	Leyland Lynx LX112TL11ZR1R	Leyland					B49F	1989	Ex Harrogate & District, 1993
240	E840EUT	Leyland Lynx LX112TL11ZR1R	Leyland					B51F	1987	Ex County, 1990
258	F358JVS	Leyland Lynx LX112TL11ZR1	Leyland					B49F	1988	Ex Jubilee, Stevenage, 1989
259	F359JVS	Leyland Lynx LX112TL11ZR1	Leyland					B49F	1988	Ex County, 1990
271	E371YRO	Leyland Lynx LX112TL11ZR1	Leyland					B51F	1987	Ex County, 1990
284	G384MWX	Leyland Lynx LX112L10ZR1R	Leyland					DP47F	1990	Ex Harrogate & District, 1995
296	G296KWY	Leyland Lynx LX112L10ZR1R	Leyland					B49F	1989	Ex Harrogate & District, 1997
297	G297KWY	Leyland Lynx LX112L10ZR1R	Leyland					B49F	1989	Ex Harrogate & District, 1997
316	P316RGS	Volvo B10M-62	Plaxton Première 350					C53F	1996	
317	P317RGS	Volvo B10M-62	Plaxton Première 350					C53F	1996	
318	P318RGS	Volvo B10M-62	Plaxton Première 350					C53F	1996	

325	F425DUG	Volvo B10M-60	Plaxton Paramount 3200 3				C50F	1989	Ex Cambridge Coach Services, 1996
327	H627UWR	Volvo B10M-60	Plaxton Paramount 3500 3				C50F	1991	Ex Wallace Arnold, Leeds, 1993
328	H628UWR	Volvo B10M-60	Plaxton Paramount 3500 3				C50F	1991	Ex Wallace Arnold, Leeds, 1993
349	J749RWT	Volvo B10M-60	Plaxton Première 350				C50F	1992	Ex Cambridge Coach Services, 1996
403	H403FGS	Mercedes-Benz 811D	Reeve Burgess				B31F	1991	Ex Sovereign (Harrow), 1995
404	H404FGS	Mercedes-Benz 811D	Reeve Burgess				B31F	1990	Ex Sovereign (Harrow), 1995
433	K3SBC	Mercedes-Benz 811D	Plaxton				B31F	1993	Ex Welwyn & Hatfield, 1996
434	K4SBC	Mercedes-Benz 811D	Plaxton				B31F	1993	Ex Welwyn & Hatfield, 1996

442-452		Mercedes-Benz 811D	Plaxton				B31F	1993/4	

442	L2SBC	444	L944MTM	446	L946MTM	448	L948MTM	450	L950MBH	452	L952MBH
443	L3SBC	445	L945MTM	447	L947MTM	449	L949MBH	451	L951MBH		

521	FUG321T	Leyland National 10351B/1R					B44F	1979	Ex Keighley & District, 1994
525	FUG325T	Leyland National 10351B/1R					B44F	1979	Ex Keighley & District, 1995
601	P601RGS	Volvo B6LE	Wright Crusader				B38F	1997	
864	B264KPF	Leyland Tiger TRCTL11/2RH	Plaxton Paramount 3200 2				C49F	1985	Ex Keighley & District, 1995

901-917		Mercedes-Benz 709D	Reeve Burgess				B23F	1989	901/2/4-6/8 ex Welwyn & Hatfield, 1996; 915 ex County, 1991

901	G901UPP	903	G903UPP	905	G905UPP	908	G908UPP	916	G916UPP
902	G902UPP	904	G904UPP	906	G906UPP	915	G915UPP	917	G917UPP

920	H920FGS	Mercedes-Benz 709D	Reeve Burgess	B23F	1990	Ex Sovereign (Harrow), 1996
990	K390SLB	Mercedes-Benz 709D	Plaxton	B23F	1993	
991	K391SLB	Mercedes-Benz 709D	Plaxton	B23F	1993	
992	K392SLB	Mercedes-Benz 709D	Plaxton	B23F	1993	Ex Welwyn & Hatfield, 1996
993	K393SLB	Mercedes-Benz 709D	Plaxton	B23F	1993	Ex Welwyn & Hatfield, 1996

Vehicle on loan

501	P501VRO	Dennis Dart SFD	Plaxton Pointer	B39F	1997	Demonstrator

On order

6 Volvo B6LE - Wright single-deckers.

Special liveries

Allover advertisements: 37, 258, 916
Green Line: 316-8/25/49
Jetlink 747: 327/8
London Sovereign: 33
Welwyn-Hatfield Line: 215, 433/4, 901/2/4-8/92/3

SPEEDLINK

| AC1-8 | | Mercedes-Benz 814D | | Autobus Classique Nouvelle | | | C24F | 1996 | | | | | |

| 1 | N100SAS | 3 | N300SAS | 5 | N500SAS | 7 | N700SAS |
| 2 | N200SAS | 4 | N400SAS | 6 | N600SAS | 8 | N800SAS |

D1	P111SAS	DAF DE33WSSB3000	Van Hool Alizée	C35FT	1997
D2	P222SAS	DAF DE33WSSB3000	Van Hool Alizée	C35FT	1997
D3	P333SAS	DAF DE33WSSB3000	Van Hool Alizée	C35FT	1997
D4	P444SAS	DAF DE33WSSB3000	Van Hool Alizée	C35FT	1997

| D13-19 | | DAF DE33WSSB3000 | | Plaxton Première 350 | | | C51FT | 1997 | | | | | |

| 13 | P30SAS | 14 | P40SAS | 15 | P50SAS | 16 | P60SAS | 17 | P70SAS | 18 | P80SAS | 19 | P90SAS |

| S1-20 | | Scania K113CRB | | Van Hool Alizée | | | C35FT* | 1992-95 | * S9 is C37FT | | | | |

1	J111SAS	4	J444SAS	7	K77SAS	10	K100SAS	13	L3SAS	16	M716KPD	19	M719KPD
2	J222SAS	5	J555SAS	8	K88SAS	11	L10SAS	14	L4SAS	17	M717KPD	20	M720KPD
3	J333SAS	6	K66SAS	9	K99SAS	12	L2SAS	15	L5SAS	18	M718KPD		

S25	N825DKU	Scania K113CRB	Van Hool Alizée	C35FT	1996
S26	N826DKU	Scania K113CRB	Van Hool Alizée	C35FT	1996
S27	N827DKU	Scania K113CRB	Van Hool Alizée	C35FT	1996
S28	N828DKU	Scania K113CRB	Van Hool Alizée	C35FT	1996
S29	N829DKU	Scania K113CRB	Van Hool Alizée	C35FT	1996
S44	L44SAS	Scania K93CRB	Plaxton Première 320	C47FT	1993
S55	L55SAS	Scania K93CRB	Plaxton Première 320	C47FT	1993

| V3-17 | | Volvo B10M-60 | | Plaxton | | | C49F* | 1990 | * V3-5 are C37F; V8/9 are C44F | | | | |

| 3 | G803BPG | 5u | G805BPG | 7 | G807BPG | 9w | G809BPG | 14 | G814BPG | 16 | G816BPG |
| 4 | G804BPG | 6 | G806BPG | 8w | G808BPG | 12 | G812BPG | 15 | G815BPG | 17 | G817BPG |

V18	K80SAS	Volvo B10M-60	Plaxton Expressliner	C49FT	1993
V19	K90SAS	Volvo B10M-60	Plaxton Expressliner	C46FT	1993
V20	K200SAS	Volvo B10M-60	Plaxton Expressliner	C46FT	1993
V21	M721KPD	Volvo B10M-62	Plaxton Première 350	C51F	1995
V22	M722KPD	Volvo B10M-62	Plaxton Première 350	C51F	1995
V23	M723KPD	Volvo B10M-62	Plaxton Première 350	C51F	1995
V24	M724KPD	Volvo B10M-62	Plaxton Première 350	C51F	1995
V25	M725KPD	Volvo B10M-62	Plaxton Première 350	C51F	1995

H32	F134UMD	Mercedes-Benz 709D	Reeve Burgess	C12FL	1989	Ex Capital, West Drayton, 1995

181-198		Dennis Lance SLF 11SDA3205*		Berkhof				B37D		1995		* 181-8 are 11SDA3206	
181	M181UAN	184	M184UAN	187	M187UAN	190	M190UAN	193	M193UAN	196	M196UAN		
182	M182UAN	185	M185UAN	188	M188UAN	191	M191UAN	194	M194UAN	197	M197UAN		
183	M183UAN	186	M186UAN	189	M189UAN	192	M192UAN	195	M195UAN	198	M198UAN		

226-251		Volvo B6LE-53		Wright				DP30F		1997			
226	P226AAP	230	P230AAP	234	P234AAP	238	P238AAP	242	P242AAP	246	P246AAP	250	P250AAP
227	P227AAP	231	P231AAP	235	P235AAP	239	P239AAP	243	P243AAP	247	P247AAP	251	P251AAP
228	P228AAP	232	P232AAP	236	P236AAP	240	P240AAP	244	P244AAP	248	P248AAP		
229	P229AAP	233	P233AAP	237	P237AAP	241	P241AAP	245	P245AAP	249	P249AAP		

901-910		DAF SB220LT550		Northern Counties Paladin				B49F		1996	
901	P901PWW	903	P903PWW	905	P905PWW	907	P907PWW	909	P909PWW		
902	P902PWW	904	P904PWW	906	P906PWW	908	P908PWW	910	P910PWW		

911	P911PWW	Dennis Dart SFD212BR1		Wright				B36F		1996
912	P912PWW	Dennis Dart SFD212BR1		Wright				B36F		1996

957-968		Dennis Lance SLF 11SDA3205		Berkhof		B33D		1995
957	M957SDP	959	M959SDP	965	M965SDP	967	M967SDP	
958	M958SDP	964	M964SDP	966	M966SDP	968	M968SDP	

971-989		DAF DE02GSSB220		Plaxton Prestige				B31D		1997			
971	R971FNW	974	R974FNW	977	R977FNW	980	R980FNW	983	R983FNW	986	R986FNW	989	R989FNW
972	R972FNW	975	R975FNW	978	R978FNW	981	R981FNW	984	R984FNW	987	R987FNW		
973	R973FNW	976	R976FNW	979	R979FNW	982	R982FNW	985	R985FNW	988	R988FNW		

Special liveries

Blue: AC6-8.
Flightline: V6/7/12/4-7.
Heathrow Hotel Hoppa: 226-51.
Heathrow Fast Train: 971-89.
Jetlink: S25-9/44/5, V8/9/13/8-25.
Speedlink Gatwick: D1-4, S6-20, V3/4.
Virgin Atlantic: AC1/3/4.
White: AC2/5, 901-12.
Woking Railair: S1-5.

On order

5 DAF-Plaxton C—F.

THX261S	Leyland National 10351A/2R	East Lancs Greenway (1993)	B41F	1978	Ex London Buses, 1992
EUI4415	Volvo B10M-61	Berkhof	C49FT	1983	Ex Time, Thornton Heath, 1995
B761OPJ	Mercedes-Benz L608D	Reeve Burgess	DP21F	1984	Ex Chivers, Elstead, 1995
HIL6246	Leyland Tiger TRCTL11/3RH	Berkhof Everest 370	C53F	1986	Ex Speedlink, 1996
F930TBP	Mercedes-Benz 609D	Reeve Burgess	DP24F	1989	Ex van, 1995
G472PGE	Leyland Lynx LX112L10ZR1R	Leyland	B51F	1989	Ex Whitelaw, Stonehouse, 1993
H748CBP	Mercedes-Benz 811D	Phoenix Eagle	B33F	1990	Ex Hertfordshire County Council (npsv), 1992
H840NOC	Dennis Dart 9.8SDL3004	Carlyle Dartline	B43F	1991	Ex Hertfordshire County Council (npsv), 1992
H849NOC	Dennis Dart 9.8SDL3004	Carlyle Dartline	B43F	1991	Ex Hertfordshire County Council (npsv), 1992
M47HUT	Blue Bird RE	Blue Bird	B51F	1994	
M48HUT	Blue Bird RE	Blue Bird	B51F	1994	
M49HUT	Blue Bird RE	Blue Bird	B51F	1994	
M51HUT	Blue Bird RE	Blue Bird	B51F	1994	
M527UGS	Mercedes-Benz OH1416	Wright Urbanranger	B47F	1995	
M255UKX	Mercedes-Benz OH1416	Wright Urbanranger	B47F	1995	
M146VVS	Dennis Dart 9.8SDL3054	Wright Handybus	B42F	1995	
M148VVS	Dennis Dart 9.8SDL3054	Wright Handybus	B42F	1995	
N421ENM	Dennis Dart 9.8SDL3054	Marshall C37	B40F	1995	
N422ENM	Dennis Dart 9.8SDL3054	Marshall C37	B40F	1995	
N423ENM	Dennis Dart 9.8SDL3054	Marshall C37	B40F	1995	
N424ENM	Dennis Dart 9.8SDL3054	Marshall C37	B40F	1995	
P664PNM	Dennis Dart SFD322BR1	Wright Crusader	B41F	1996	
P665PNM	Dennis Dart SFD322BR1	Wright Crusader	B41F	1996	
P667PNM	Dennis Dart SFD322BR1	Wright Crusader	B41F	1996	
P668PNM	Dennis Dart SFD322BR1	Wright Crusader	B41F	1996	
P647SBH	Dennis Dart SFD322BR1	Wright Crusader	B31F	1996	Ex Wright, Belfast (demonstrator), 1997
P980PTM	Marshall Midibus	Marshall	B29F	1996	
R649VBM	Dennis Dart SFD322BR1	Wright Crusader	B41F	1997	
R650VBM	Dennis Dart SFD322BR1	Wright Crusader	B41F	1997	
R651VBM	Dennis Dart SFD322BR1	Wright Crusader	B41F	1997	
R652VBM	Dennis Dart SFD322BR1	Wright Crusader	B41F	1997	
R653VBM	Dennis Dart SFD322BR1	Wright Crusader	B41F	1997	
R654VBM	Dennis Dart SFD322BR1	Wright Crusader	B41F	1997	
"XVA444"	Dennis Dart SFD322BR1	Wright Crusader	B41F	1997	

Previous registrations

B761OPB	B967MLF, KXI599	**EUI4415**	BDV862Y	**HIL6246**	C146SPB

Special liveries

Overall advertisements : H840/9NOC

A124EPA	Arriva Southend 563	HIL2279	Arriva Kent & Sussex 2841	R455SKX	Arriva The Shires 4055
A141EPA	Arriva Southend 553	HIL7595	Arriva The Shires 4015	R456SKX	Arriva The Shires 4056
A143EPA	Arriva The Shires 4008	HIL7597	Arriva The Shires 4027	R201VPU	Arriva Herts & Essex PDL201
A150EPA	Arriva The Shires 4010	H845AHS	Arriva Southend 565	R202VPU	Arriva Herts & Essex PDL202
A152EPA	Arriva The Shires 4002	H846AHS	Arriva Kent & Sussex 2846	R203VPU	Arriva Herts & Essex PDL203
A153EPA	Arriva The Shires 4003	H847AHS	Arriva Kent & Sussex 2847	R204VPU	Arriva Herts & Essex PDL204
A155EPA	Arriva The Shires 4005	H566MPD	Arriva Southend 566	R205VPU	Arriva Herts & Essex PDL205
A14GTA	Arriva Kent & Sussex 2845	H567MPD	Arriva Southend 567	R206VPU	Arriva Herts & Essex PDL206
A246SVW	Arriva Southend 546	H372PHK	Arriva Southend 568	R207VPU	Arriva Herts & Essex PDL207
A247SVW	Arriva Southend 547	H616UWR	Arriva Kent & Sussex 2848	R208VPU	Arriva Herts & Essex PDL208
A248SVW	Arriva Southend 548	H618UWR	Arriva Kent & Sussex 2849	R209VPU	Arriva Herts & Essex PDL209
A249SVW	Arriva Southend 549	J749RWT	Sovereign 349	SIB4846	Arriva The Shires 4016
B292KPF	Arriva The Shires 4012	P316RGS	Sovereign 316	SIB7480	Arriva The Shires 4020
B293KPF	Arriva The Shires 4013	P317RGS	Sovereign 317	SIB8529	Arriva The Shires 4025
B835SWX	Arriva Southend 557	P318RGS	Sovereign 318	TIB5901	Arriva Kent & Sussex 2844
B845SWX	Arriva Southend 558	R903BKO	Arriva Kent & Sussex 2903	TJI4820	The Bee Line VJ790
B855SWX	Arriva Southend 559	R904BKO	Arriva Kent & Sussex 2904	TJI4822	The Bee Line VJ782
B100XTW	Arriva Southend 551	R905BKO	Arriva Kent & Sussex 2905	TJI4823	The Bee Line VJ783
C254SPC	Arriva Herts & Essex TDL54	R906BKO	Arriva Kent & Sussex 2906	TJI4826	The Bee Line VJ786
C255SPC	Arriva Herts & Essex TDL55	R907BKO	Arriva Kent & Sussex 2907	TJI4828	The Bee Line VJ788
C260SPC	Arriva Herts & Essex TDL60	R908BKO	Arriva Kent & Sussex 2908	TJI4829	The Bee Line VJ789
C147SPE	Arriva The Shires 4017	R909BKO	Arriva Kent & Sussex 2909	TJI4830	The Bee Line SB740
C149SPE	Arriva The Shires 4019	R910BKO	Arriva Kent & Sussex 2910	TJI4831	The Bee Line SB741
E881KKY	Arriva The Shires 4021	R447SKX	Arriva The Shires 4047	TJI4832	The Bee Line SB742
E882KKY	Arriva The Shires 4022	R448SKX	Arriva The Shires 4048	TJI4833	The Bee Line SB743
E323OMG	Arriva The Shires 4023	R449SKX	Arriva The Shires 4049	TJI4834	The Bee Line SB744
F425DUG	Sovereign 325	R450SKX	Arriva The Shires 4050	TJI4835	The Bee Line SB745
F572UPB	Arriva Southend 572	R451SKX	Arriva The Shires 4051	TJI4836	The Bee Line SB746
F425UVW	Arriva Southend 569	R452SKX	Arriva The Shires 4052	TJI4838	The Bee Line TP768
F467UVW	Arriva Southend 570	R453SKX	Arriva The Shires 4053	TIB5906	Arriva The Shires 4046
F523UVW	Arriva Southend 571	R454SKX	Arriva The Shires 4054		

GREEN LINE Vehicles in numerical order of fleet number

ARRIVA HERTS & ESSEX

TDL54	C254SPC	Leyland Tiger TRCTL11/3RH	Duple 320	C53F	1986	Ex London & Country, 1993
TDL55	C255SPC	Leyland Tiger TRCTL11/3RH	Duple 320	C49F	1986	Ex London & Country, 1993
TDL60	C260SPC	Leyland Tiger TRCTL11/3RH	Duple 320	C49F	1986	Ex London & Country, 1993

PDL201-209 DAF DE02GGSB220 Plaxton Prestige DP37F 1997

201	R201VPU	**203**	R203VPU	**205**	R205VPU	**207**	R207VPU	**209** R209VPU
202	R202VPU	**204**	R204VPU	**206**	R206VPU	**208**	R208VPU	

SOVEREIGN

316	P316RGS	Volvo B10M-62	Plaxton Première 350	C53F	1996	
317	P317RGS	Volvo B10M-62	Plaxton Première 350	C53F	1996	
318	P318RGS	Volvo B10M-62	Plaxton Première 350	C53F	1996	
325	F425DUG	Volvo B10M-60	Plaxton Paramount 3200 3	C50F	1989	Ex Cambridge Coach Services, 1996
349	J749RWT	Volvo B10M-60	Plaxton Première 350	C50F	1992	Ex Cambridge Coach Services, 1996

ARRIVA SOUTHEND

546	A246SVW	Leyland Tiger TRCTL11/3RP	Duple	C57F	1984	
547	A247SVW	Leyland Tiger TRCTL11/3RP	Duple	C57F	1984	
548	A248SVW	Leyland Tiger TRCTL11/3RP	Duple	C57F	1984	
549	A249SVW	Leyland Tiger TRCTL11/3RP	Duple	C57F	1984	
551	B100XTW	Leyland Tiger TRCTL11/3RP	Duple	C51F	1984	
553	A141EPA	Leyland Tiger TRCTL11/3R	Plaxton Paramount 3200 Exp	C57F	1984	Ex London Country South West, 1990
557	B83SWX	Leyland Tiger TRCTL11/3RH	Plaxton Paramount 3.00 2 Exp	C57F	1985	Ex Yorkshire Voyager, Leeds, 1990
558	B84SWX	Leyland Tiger TRCTL11/3RH	Plaxton Paramount 3.00 2 Exp	C57F	1985	Ex Yorkshire Voyager, Leeds, 1990
559	B85SWX	Leyland Tiger TRCTL11/3RH	Plaxton Paramount 3.00 2 Exp	C53F	1985	Ex Yorkshire Voyager, Leeds, 1990
563	A124EPA	Leyland Tiger TRCTL11/2RH	Plaxton Paramount 3200 Exp	C53F	1983	Ex Kentish Bus, 1990
565	H845AHS	Volvo B10M-60	Plaxton	C53F	1991	Ex Express Travel, Speke, 1995
566	H566MPD	Volvo B10M-60	Plaxton	C53F	1991	Ex Express Travel, Speke, 1995
567	H567MPD	Volvo B10M-60	Plaxton	C53F	1991	Ex Express Travel, Speke, 1995
568	H372PHK	Volvo B10M-60	Plaxton	C53F	1991	Ex Express Travel, Speke, 1995
569	F425UVW	Volvo B10M-60	Plaxton	C53F	1989	Ex Express Travel, Speke, 1995
570	F467UVW	Volvo B10M-60	Plaxton	C53F	1989	Ex Express Travel, Speke, 1995
571	F523UVW	Volvo B10M-60	Plaxton	C53F	1989	Ex Express Travel, Speke, 1995
572	F572UPB	Volvo B10M-60	Plaxton	C53F	1989	Ex Express Travel, Speke, 1995

THE BEE LINE

SB740-746 Scania K113CRB Berkhof Excellence 1000 C53F 1995

740	TJI4830	**741**	TJI4831	**742**	TJI4832	**743**	TJI4833	**744**	TJI4834	**745**	TJI 4835	**746**	TJI4836

TP768	TJI4838	Leyland Tiger TRCTL11/3R	Plaxton Paramount 3200 3	C53F	1988	Ex Luton & District, 1993
VJ782	TJI4822	Volvo B10M-60	Jonckheere Jubilee P50	C53F	1989	Ex Alder Valley, 1992
VJ783	TJI4823	Volvo B10M-60	Jonckheere Jubilee P50	C53F	1989	Ex Alder Valley, 1992
VJ786	TJI4826	Volvo B10M-60	Jonckheere Jubilee P50	C53F	1989	Ex Alder Valley, 1992
VJ788	TJI4828	Volvo B10M-60	Jonckheere Jubilee P50	C53F	1989	Ex Alder Valley, 1992
VJ789	TJI4829	Volvo B10M-60	Jonckheere Jubilee P50	C53F	1989	Ex Alder Valley, 1992
VJ790	TJI4820	Volvo B10M-60	Jonckheere Jubilee P50	C53F	1989	

ARRIVA KENT & SUSSEX

2841	HIL2279	Volvo B10M-61	Plaxton Paramount 3500 3	C50F	1988	Ex Kentish Bus, 1997
2844	TIB5901	Volvo B10M-61	Plaxton Paramount 3500 3	C50F	1988	Ex Kentish Bus, 1997
2845	A14GTA	Volvo B10M-62	Plaxton Paramount 3500 3	C49FT	1990	Ex New Enterprise, Maidstone, 1997
2846	H846AHS	Volvo B10M-60	Plaxton Paramount 3500 3	C49FT	1991	Ex Express Travel, Speke, 1995
2847	H847AHS	Volvo B10M-60	Plaxton Paramount 3500 3	C51F	1991	Ex Express Travel, Speke, 1995
2848	H616UWR	Volvo B10M-60	Plaxton Paramount 3500 3	C50F	1991	Ex Wilson, Paisley, 1996
2849	H618UWR	Volvo B10M-60	Plaxton Paramount 3500 3	C50F	1991	Ex Berkeley, Paulton, 1996

2903-2910		DAF SB3000	Plaxton Prima	C53F	1998

2903	R903BKO	**2905**	R905BKO	**2907**	R907BKO	**2909**	R909BKO
2904	R904BKO	**2906**	R906BKO	**2908**	R908BKO	**2910**	R910BKO

ARRIVA THE SHIRES

4002	A152EPA	Leyland Tiger TRCTL11/3R	Plaxton Paramount 3200 Exp	C57F	1984	Ex London Country North West, 1990
4003	A153EPA	Leyland Tiger TRCTL11/3R	Plaxton Paramount 3200 Exp	C53F	1984	Ex London Country North West, 1990
4005	A155EPA	Leyland Tiger TRCTL11/3R	Plaxton Paramount 3200 Exp	C53F	1984	Ex London Country North West, 1990
4008	A143EPA	Leyland Tiger TRCTL11/3R	Plaxton Paramount 3200 Exp	C51F	1984	Ex London Country North West, 1990
4010	A150EPA	Leyland Tiger TRCTL11/3R	Plaxton Paramount 3200 Exp	C51F	1984	Ex London Country North West, 1990
4012	B292KPF	Leyland Tiger TRCTL11/3RH	Plaxton Paramount 3200 2	C51F	1985	Ex London Country North West, 1990
4013	B293KPF	Leyland Tiger TRCTL11/3RH	Plaxton Paramount 3200 2	C51F	1985	Ex London Country North West, 1990
4015	HIL7595	Volvo B10M-61		C53F	1988	Ex Moor-Dale, Newcastle, 1994
4016	SIB4846	Leyland Tiger TRCTL11/3ARZA	Plaxton	C53F	1988	
4017	C147SPE	Leyland Tiger TRCTL11/3RH	Berkhof Everest 370	C53F	1986	Ex London Country North West, 1990
4019	C149SPE	Leyland Tiger TRCTL11/3RH	Berkhof Everest 370	C53F	1986	Ex London Country North West, 1990
4020	SIB7480	Leyland Tiger TRCL10/3ARZA	Plaxton	C51FT	1988	Ex London Country North West, 1990
4021	E881KKY	Leyland Tiger TRCTL11/3ARZ	Plaxton	C53F	1988	
4022	E882KKY	Leyland Tiger TRCTL11/3ARZ	Plaxton	C53F	1988	
4023	E323OMG	Leyland Tiger TRCTL11/3ARZA	Plaxton Paramount 3200 3	C53F	1988	Ex London Country North West, 1990
4025	SIB8529	Leyland Tiger TRCL10/3ARZA	Plaxton	C51FT	1988	Ex London Country North West, 1990
4027	HIL7597	Volvo B10M-61	Plaxton	C53F	1988	Ex Moor-Dale, Newcastle, 1994
4046	TIB5906	Leyland Tiger TRCTL11/3RH	Duple 320	C51F	1986	Ex Kentish Bus, 1997

4047-4056		DAF DE33WSSB3000	Plaxton Première 320	C53F	1997

4047	R447SKX	**4049**	R449SKX	**4051**	R451SKX	**4053**	R453SKX	**4055**	R455SKX
4048	R448SKX	**4050**	R450SKX	**4052**	R452SKX	**4054**	R454SKX	**4056**	R456SKX

NOTES

NOTES

NOTES